ALCOHOL FREEDOM

7 Powerful Mindsets to Kickstart Your Alcohol-Free Journey

BY
KEVIN O'HARA

A Unique, Free, Online Quit-Alcohol Resource
Visit: AlcoholMastery.com

Alcohol Freedom

This book is not intended as a substitute for the medical advice of physicians. The reader should regularly consult a physician in matters relating to his/her health and particularly with respect to any symptoms that may require diagnosis or medical attention.

First edition, 2015

Stihlman Publishing
Rojales
Alicante
ISBN-13: 978-1511611527

ISBN-10: 1511611529

For Bernard
Thanks for everything, Dad!
I love you always x

Contents

Introduction

Welcome to *Alcohol Freedom, 7 Powerful Mindsets to Kickstart Your Alcohol-Free Journey!* This book is for anyone who wants to quit drinking alcohol but doesn't know how to get started. If that is you, I can understand something of what you are feeling. A little over two years ago, as I write these words, I was in a similar position to the one you are in now. What I've learned in those two years will help you to avoid a lot of unnecessary pain and suffering. If I had only five minutes to speak to you, my message would be simple: You are *not* an alcoholic. You have built a bad habit involving alcohol over many years, but that bad habit can be torn to shreds in a matter of weeks by changing the some of the ways you think. Luckily, because you have bought this book, I have a bit more than five minutes to deliver my message.

I would love to be able to tell you that before I quit drinking alcohol I had this wonderful epiphany, showing me the one way of beating my alcohol habit. It wasn't like that. My drinking had been worrying me for a long time before I finally stopped. For the most part, I had been thinking about how I could cut down. I didn't want to quit. Maybe I could only drink over the weekends, with meals, or while I was watching the football. But I've had these thoughts about restricting my alcohol use enough times to know that I couldn't control anything about my drinking. I'd follow that path for a few weeks, holding tight to my own controls. Then gradually I'd let go a little here, a bit more there, and soon I would be right back where I started: drinking alcohol whenever and wherever I felt like it.

Although I didn't have that initial flash of insight, there *was* one single event that helped to finally make up my mind to quit. I talked about this in my first book, ***How to Stop Drinking Alcohol.*** I only got to see my son two or three times a year. Each of those occasions was treated like a good old fashioned celebration. In my world, celebrations always meant plenty of food and alcohol. The year I quit, I had just spent over a week 'celebrating' with my son. By the time he returned home, at the end of his vacation, I had spent a small fortune and had no great memories to show for it. In fact, I didn't have many memories. They were all lost to the alcohol smog. Thinking about this in the long term, I realized that every time I met my son in the future would end in similar circumstances. What a crappy way to live. I decided to quit, but I hadn't got a clue *how* I was actually going to do it!

On average, we live about twenty seven thousand days on this planet. Not very many when it's put like that, is it! Since I was a teenager, my alcohol habit had been slowly snipping away at the edges of those twenty seven thousand days. I had already spent a huge block of that time being wasted on booze and I didn't want to waste any more.

When I reached the conclusion that I had to quit for good, I felt frightened and isolated. I was completely ashamed about the person I had become, the drunk or the alcoholic. I felt like a loser. I felt like an outsider in my own world because, as far as I was concerned, I was the only person who had this problem.

I was scared because I wasn't sure if I could have a normal life again. Had I gone too far with my drinking? Would I be able to rise above this and stop using alcohol completely? How long would it take? How would I feel? What damage had I caused to myself? What damage had I caused to my relationships? What would happen to my social life? I had so many questions and not very many good answers.

I imagined that once my 'alcoholism' was made public, people would be talking about me behind my back. I dreaded the humiliation that I would feel every time I had to refuse a glass of wine at a meal or sit watching a football match with an orange juice, while all my buddies were enjoying their ice cold pints of beer.

I felt pissed off and cheated because, once I quit, I would be depriving myself of something that genuinely gave me great pleasure.

It was just a lousy situation to be in. I knew I really needed to stop the destruction. How I was living my life was beyond the joke and there was no way I could hide from the consequences of drinking so much alcohol anymore. But being a drinker still felt like such a natural part of my life, of who I was as a person.

The truth is that when I quit I did feel humiliated. I did feel deprived, and I did feel that some people were talking behind my back, calling me an alcoholic, or worse. That really hurt me. The pitying looks, the jokes, and the remarks were all real and they made me feel like crap. I felt like I had completely let myself and my family down. It almost drove me back to the drink.

But that was in the beginning. Each day that went by without drinking alcohol made my body and mind feel stronger and sharper. The humiliation and the thoughts about being deprived didn't last long because there was no substance behind them. What I realized was that these thoughts were just a part of the drinkers mentality that I had built up over many years. We all get suckered into the propaganda and the lies about how alcohol is a normal part of life. How could I feel deprived when I was feeling happier than I had felt in a very long time. Far from being humiliated, I was elated and raring to go. I knew I had wasted so many years on this pathetic drug, but that all in the past.

The mindsets that I have set out for you in this book will help you to pull back and view your alcohol drinking from a much wider perspective. You will be able to see behavior patterns that other people cannot see. The simplest, easiest, and most efficient way of making changes in your life is by changing the how you think. If you change one aspect of your thinking, that change will have a knock-on effect that can alter your whole life. These changes are simple shifts in your perspective, alternative ways of looking at things.

I'm so excited that you have chosen me to be your guide through this exciting time in your life. These mindsets have changed my life and given me a strong belief in who I am and in my abilities to create my own future. I hope they will do the same for you.

I'm Kevin O'Hara of Alcohol Mastery...

Let's go onwards and upwards!

Alcohol Freedom Mindset One

Quitting Drinking is 5% of What Happens To You and 95% How You Respond

"You can have all the tools in the world but if you don't genuinely believe in yourself, it's useless."
Ken Jeong

You are about to start a new chapter in your life. To stop drinking alcohol is only the first sentence of the first paragraph of that first chapter. The process of quitting alcohol doesn't take years, months, weeks, or even days - it's over in a moment. Imagine stepping through a doorway and closing the door behind you. It's as simple as that. If you decide, right now, *in this very moment*, to never use alcohol again... you've succeeded - Congratulations! You've done it! You've just quit alcohol and there is no more to it than that.

At the heart of any habit, there is a fundamental core that holds the whole structure together. Imagine that your habit is a hot air balloon drifting across the sky. What is it that keeps that balloon from crashing down to earth in a crumpled heap? Heat! A gas burner heats the air inside the balloon, the hot air rises, which takes the surrounding balloon with it up into the atmosphere. If you turn off the burner, thereby taking away the heat source, the whole structure collapses and sinks to the ground.

Building Your Habit

In a similar fashion, any habit is fundamentally built around a single core behavior. A drug habit is built around the behavior of taking a particular drug. A chocolate habit is built around the behavior of eating loads of chocolate. A running habit is built around running. A nose-picking habit is built around picking your nose. A teeth-brushing habit is built around the habit of brushing your teeth. Your alcohol habit is built around your behavior of drinking alcohol. Removing any of these behaviors means that the structure of the habit cannot survive.

Just taking the alcohol out of the habit doesn't mean the habit is gone from your life. There are still going to be companies that make alcohol, places that sell alcohol, advertisements for the various alcohol brands, and other people who drink alcohol. You have no control over any of this. Your control lies in what you put into your body. It doesn't matter how much alcohol there is in the world, if you control the behavior of drinking the alcohol, you'll never have an alcohol problem again. Of course, there are still plenty of other less harmful uses for alcohol. You can use it as a fuel, an industrial solvent, or a cleaner.

So from your point of view, the only thing that's holding your alcohol habit together is not the alcohol, but your alcohol-drinking behavior. This is a major distinction. A person who blames the alcohol is merely deflecting attention away from themselves, from their drinking thoughts, and from the very behavior that lies at the root cause of their problems. The alcohol is merely the tool you use to get the end result you want. If a person stabs someone with a knife, you don't lock up the knife. Blaming alcohol instead of yourself as the drinker means you're likely to stay on the same destructive path.

On the other hand, the person who understands that the entire alcohol habit is structured around the behavior of putting alcohol into their bodies, mouthful after mouthful, can change the entire

ALCOHOL FREEDOM • 7

course of their lives by changing the behavior. Without drinking the alcohol, the habit cannot hold itself together. Just as a hot air balloon cannot stay afloat without heat, the alcohol habit without the alcohol-drinking behavior will collapse.

The Drinking Life Desire

Just as a balloon can be kept afloat by replacing the hot air with another buoyant gas, you can also do a really good job of keeping the structure of your alcohol habit artificially inflated by pumping in a lot of psychological 'hot air'. For instance, you can keep it afloat by telling yourself that you're an alcoholic and you'll never be free from the 'demon drink'. You can tell yourself that alcoholism is in your genes, in your family, or that drinking alcohol is a part of your cultural identity. Even long after the last vestiges of alcohol have disappeared from your system, you can keep the alcohol addiction alive and well through your thoughts and perceptions. Even though the alcohol flow has stopped, the desire for the drinking lifestyle is still strong.

If you don't *want* to quit, you never will, no matter how long you go without actually drinking alcohol. To reach permanent alcohol freedom, you must kill the desire for drinking this toxin. Alcohol Mastery is a free online resource I've set up to help you kill that desire. You can find out more by visiting alcoholmastery.com.

Can you recognize that your alcohol habit has been caused by each mouthful of alcohol, that nobody forced you to drink, and that each drink was completely under your control? Are you beginning to recognize that all those changes you now need to make in your life have absolutely nothing to do with the alcohol once you don't drink anymore?

Some people say that they cannot control their drinking, that once they have that first drink in a session, they can't stop. The reality is that once they start, they don't want to stop. There's a big difference between can't and won't.

What to Expect from This Book

This quick introduction to the ideas of Alcohol Mastery will give you a few simple techniques to dismantle or re-purpose those alcohol habit structures. Once you've worked your way through this book, you will have enough ammunition to begin breaking down those limiting beliefs and values that have brought you to where you are now. You will also learn some skills to begin laying those all-important foundational stones on which you will base all your future success.

These techniques will help you to quickly overcome your alcohol drug habit. They will also help you to effectively deal with any other bad habits that are lurking in the darker recesses of your mind. Additionally, the tools and techniques with which you rid yourself of this bad habit are essentially the same ones that will help you to build the constructive habits that are the foundation of your success.

We all have problems. That's just a part of life. The most common way of trying to solve these problems is to look for easy, external solutions. We often seek out people who can offer us quick fixes that take very little effort on our part. We want a 'buy-now-pay-later' ticket away from our difficulties and into lifelong happiness.

How much would you be willing to pay to get your hands on that one piece of essential advice that would alter your life forever? Or how much would you fork out for a wonder drug that would magically cure all your problems with one simple dose? All you have to do is take the pill, go to sleep, and wake up happy, healthy, with your new life awaiting you. Some of us will read book after book, attend seminar after seminar, searching for that single perfect solution that will lead us to our personal promised land. If it were that easy, everyone would already be doing it!

On Being Your Own Teacher

ALL the answers to ALL your problems can only really be found inside your own mind. I'm not suggesting that there's a hidden chamber within the deep recesses of your brain, a cerebral Aladdin's cave, where nicely-packaged answers are waiting to be found. We all need help from time to time, but external help will only take you so far.

Outside help is great for opening your mind to other possibilities or giving you a deeper understanding of the best direction for you to take. But any external help - whether in the form of teacher, coach, book, audio, or seminar - can only take you to the threshold of your own problems and no further. External teachings can open you up to a new way of doing things, but they can't take the journey for you. There are a few different reasons for this.

The first reason is that knowledge is not the same as action. You can have all the knowledge in the world, but it's worthless if you don't put it to use. Complete learning means altering your behavior. If your behavior hasn't changed, you haven't learned.

Second, nobody has the same perceptions as you. When someone gives you advice, including what you're reading here, they're teaching you how to do things based upon their perceptions, on how they see things within their own mind. Even if your perceptions are closely matched to those of your teacher, there are still going to be big differences between how your teacher perceives things and how you perceive things. Any advice they give you will have to be adapted to your own way of thinking before you can use it.

Third, not every tool or technique will work for you. One of the answers is to learn many tools and techniques. Another is to learn how to adapt a particular tool or technique so that it fits in with your way of doing things.

Only you can understand yourself with enough insight and intimacy to be able to judge how you can adapt and apply those teachings. You make the adaptations according to your life, your environment, your body, your age, your circumstances, etc. You know if a tool or a technique is working because you receive immediate feedback. You can understand exactly what's happening in real time. You also have the ability to immediately alter the course of your thinking or your actions. By changing the course of your thoughts, you alter your perceptions and control the outcomes.

Now, you might think that you don't know enough about yourself to be able to tell if something is working or not. You might tell yourself that if you understood yourself better, you wouldn't have these problems in the first place. That's just not true. We know ourselves better than anyone else can ever know us. In most cases, all we really lack are the right tools, techniques, or strategies for altering our thinking and perceptions.

Once we learn those tools, techniques, and strategies of change, as well as learn how we can operate them within our own psychology, we can quickly apply them to our thoughts and perceptions. Change your thoughts and perceptions and your actions will largely take care of themselves. Every action first requires a thought. If you control the thoughts, you control the actions.

Your Discomfort Zone

Comfort is one of the biggest enemies of change. We love comfort. It's a basic need and a state we're always pursuing. We seek to gain comfort and avoid pain in most areas of our lives. And we don't like being outside of our zone of comfort for too long. The ability to push yourself over your personal comfort boundary and into your discomfort zone is something only you can do, and it's something that needs to be done if you're serious about making these changes in your life.

As we saw at the beginning of this chapter, your ability to stop drinking both is and is not about the alcohol. Of course alcohol is your initial target because it's been the focus of your behavior for many years. Once you get to the stage of accepting that you need to quit, the alcohol seems to be the barrier that separates you from the life you want.

As soon as you pull the alcohol out of the equation, you realize that it's your thinking that's been the problem all along. The type of thinking you've been doing has resulted in the creation of habitual behavior patterns in your life that are now causing all sorts of problems. Alcohol is merely the means to your end. Now that the alcohol is gone, the whole behavioral structure will start to collapse, leaving gaps that drinking used to fill.

You used to drink after work. Now what? You used to drink when you were stressed. Now what?

A Time for Change

Now is the time for you to turn your back on alcohol and begin to fill those gaps with less harmful behavior. Think about it like a gardener pulling out the weeds and replacing them with strong healthy plants.

The first mindset is about learning a few tools that you can use to alter your thinking and perceptions. These early tools are not going to change your life, but they'll be just enough to get you over that starting line.

Once your brain has had the chance to remain alcohol-free in the first few days, alcohol can't influence your thoughts any more or interfere with those delicate chemical and electrical balances that are so essential for a fully functioning mind. Once these chemical and electrical connections are functioning properly, your thoughts and perceptions will become clearer. Your new cleaner-running brain will be much more productive, positive, and capable. Each day that goes by gives you more experience of what it's like to be free.

Getting your head in the right place means choosing how you are going to think, how you are going to react, and how you are going to feel. It means putting yourself in the driver's seat once again. You will be in complete control.

In the next section, we're going to examine some of the more common assumptions about alcohol consumption and quitting.

Your Inflexible Assumptions Serve Only to Handicap Your Progress

"The worst mistake of first contact, made throughout history by individuals on both sides of every new encounter, has been the unfortunate habit of making assumptions. It often proved fatal."
David Brin

Assumption: *The act of taking something for granted or supposing. An assumption is something that you suppose and accept as true without question or proof.*

We all create assumptions about our lives. These assumptions are not necessarily correct. Most assumptions about why we drink alcohol are based on fictions that have been passed from person to person, from our parents or our peers. The problem is, we can easily find enough *evidence* to support false assumption if we look hard enough.

My Typical Alcoholic Assumptions

I drank for well over 30 years of my life. I started when I was in my early teens and I stopped when I was in my late forties. I started out with some very basic assumptions about alcohol:

- Everyone drank alcohol
- Drinking alcohol was normal
- Alcoholics were the bums you see on the street
- It was cool to drink alcohol
- Drinking alcohol would make me feel grown up

Over the years, I had constructed many more assumptions about alcohol, drinking alcohol, and about my particular alcohol-drinking behavior, such as:

- Alcohol was part of my culture

- I needed alcohol to help me to relax
- I enjoyed drinking alcohol
- alcohol-drinking was my pastime
- Not drinking alcohol would mean I was a sissy
- I can't sleep without alcohol
- I can't enjoy myself without alcohol
- I can't socialize without alcohol

...and so on

Here are some of my previous assumptions about quitting alcohol:

- Quitting drinking is going to be hard
- Quitting drinking will hurt
- I'll become a boring bastard without alcohol
- Quitting alcohol involves going through the shakes
- Quitting alcohol will be a lifelong commitment
- I will always crave something I can never have again
- My social life will disintegrate
- I'll be getting rid of my only pleasure

...and so on

Which of these assumptions do you recognize?

The Sum of Your Five Closest Friends

Let's look at one of my basic assumptions. *Everyone drinks alcohol. Drinking alcohol is just a part of adult life.*

When all our friends drink, it's easy to arrive at the assumption that everyone drinks alcohol. As a young boy, I believed that the way to be an adult was to act out the behaviors that I saw in the adults around me. This is the way we all learn how to grow up. We choose to see the behaviors that most reflect our personal reality of 'being an adult'. We also ignore the behaviors which oppose that reality.

The reality is that *not* everyone drinks alcohol. It's only since I've stopped drinking alcohol that I've been able to get my head around this reality. I might be sitting in a busy restaurant, sipping my glass of water. I look around and it seems to me like I'm the only one who doesn't have an alcoholic drink. Everyone else is drinking beer, wine, or some other type of alcohol. It's only when I look closer that I find the non-drinkers. I never saw them before because I wasn't looking for them. I wasn't interested in finding non-drinkers. I only saw the people who shared my passion for alcohol. This blindness to the non-alcohol drinkers became wired into my brain throughout all those years as a drinker. It's one of the last vestiges of my drinker personality that still clings on.

When I drank, my five closest friends were all drinkers. In fact, they were my friends *because* we drank together, and *because* we drank in the same bars. Our whole relationship was based on drinking alcohol and not very much else. If I ever met any of my drinking buddies outside of the pub, it was always awkward. These meetings would invariably lead to the pub or the liquor store.

Now that I don't drink alcohol anymore, things are different. My friendships are revolve around other things. Most of my friends do drink alcohol, but this isn't the reason for our friendships. Some of my mates share a passion for the same football team. So we meet up in the pub for the weekend matches. I drink orange juice. Most of them drink alcohol. However, the entire friendship revolves around supporting the same team.

I have other friendships where we may occasionally meet up for a meal. I drink what I drink, and they drink what they drink, but the relationship is defined by other things.

Look at your own friendships. How do they relate to alcohol? How will they fare once alcohol is taken out of the equation?

Habitual Assumptions

Making assumptions is an essential part of our habitual thinking process. We make assumptions about the things that happen over and over in our lives and have become very familiar to the point that we don't have to consciously think about them anymore. We assume that because these things have happened the same way, so many times in the past, then they are going to continue to act the same way, forever. For example, when you turn on the tap, you assume that water will come out of it, because water always comes out of your taps, even though there's a possibility of that not happening at some point in time.

Without assumptions, habitual behavior would be impossible. They allow us to accomplish the simplest to the most complex tasks. If you do A, you know B will follow, which will be followed by C, and so on. For example, when you turn the key in your ignition, you assume your car engine will start. When the car starts and you press the clutch pedal, you assume the clutch will disengage your engine from your transmission, allowing you to push the gear lever into first. You assume that once the first gear has been correctly selected and press the accelerator, the car will move forward, and so on.

Assumptions produce familiarity, which produces comfort. We like the familiarity of our assumptions because if something is familiar there is less chance of anything bad happening. It's better to follow the well-trodden path because you can better predict what's going to be around the corner or over the hill. We are still wired for the wild. We have evolved to protect ourselves as best we can against animals that are trying to make us their dinner. In this environment, new equals fear, familiarity equals comfort. If you want to see a stark example of this in action, watch any nature documentary on herding animals. As soon as anything new arrives on the scene, the entire pack goes into fear mode. They will remain in that fear mode until the new thing is deemed not to be a threat or it moves away.

You Can Or You Can't - It's Your Belief

Making these assumptions is an integral part of our lives and most are very beneficial. Problems arise when we start making faulty assumptions. "I'm not going to look for a better job because the economy is bad and that means there'll be no better jobs to find." "I'm not going out for a walk today because it's going to rain." "Everyone drinks." "I'll always be a drinker." "I can't quit drinking because I'll have no social life." "I can't quit drinking because alcohol helps me to sleep."

Take a look at your alcohol use. What assumptions are you making? Do you believe that alcohol is part of your culture? Do you believe that you can't quit because [fill in your assumption]? Do you believe that drinking helps you to [fill in your assumption]?

What assumptions do you make about quitting drinking? For instance, do you believe that quitting will be hard? Do you believe that your social life is going to suffer?

The truth is that nobody has a crystal ball or the magical ability to predict the future. Even if you've failed to quit in the past, that's no guarantee that stopping now will be the same.

Henry Ford said *"Whether you think you can or think you can't, you're right"*.

You need to take things as they come. You'll know how you'll feel when you feel it, and no sooner. If you assume you're going to feel like crap, guess what - you'll feel like crap! If you assume that your social life will come crashing to the ground like a lead balloon - I assume you won't be socializing any time soon.

Assume the Best

If you have to make assumptions, make positive ones. There are certain things in life you should be absolutely confident about, your ability to succeed is one of them. Assume that all the changes you make in your life are under your control. Assume that these choices are the right ones for you. Assume that you're in a process that has a beginning, a middle, and an end. Assume that this is a process that can be tweaked and molded as you go along. Assume that your health and welfare are improving the longer you stay away from this poison. Assume that you're always adjusting things towards the perfect direction for you.

Take a look at something in your life that you can do with ease. Choose a skill you have, something that you can perform without really having to think about it, something you do better than most other people. Now take a look back in your life at how you developed that skill. Where did it start? What did you have to learn to be able to do it as proficiently as you can do it now? How many years of practice did it take? How difficult was it for you in the beginning?

Think about a newborn baby who has absolutely no skills except the survival skills she was born with. She can't control anything. It takes a month before she can hear properly. It takes her a month before she can use her eyes in tandem, so her eyes might be randomly wandering or even crossing over. It can take up to 8 months before she has all her sight. To her, everything is a skill that must be learned. Eventually that young baby will learn all the necessary skills she needs to know to grow into an adult. On the way to adulthood, she'll gradually learn more complex skills. Perhaps how to paint fine art, how to play and master a violin, or maybe even how to perform delicate, lifesaving brain surgery on a newborn baby.

Almost everything you do in life will start out with a measure of fear and uncertainty. With time and practice, you'll steadily move toward confidence and trust in your abilities. Learning changes incompetence into competence.

When I first quit drinking and went into one of my favorite restaurants, I found it difficult to refuse the first glass of wine I was offered. Two years later, refusing alcohol is like water off a ducks back. The difficult has become easy. I had to learn these simple skills of asking for a non-alcoholic drink, sitting with people who were drinking alcohol while I wasn't, answering questions about my non-drinking, and many others. You might never have thought about such simple things as skills that you need to learn, but that's exactly what they are. With practice and persistence, you will learn all the skills you need for your alcohol freedom.

Interestingly enough, it's this progression from difficulty to ease which prevents unhealthy and destructive habits from forming in the first place. It's through these processes of growth - making it through the difficult to the easy - that you enrich and solidify your healthy self-esteem.

Next, we'll take a look at how your assumptions can elevate your expectations.

Raising Your Expectations to Meet Your Performance

"Let your dreams outgrow the shoes of your expectations."
Ryunosuke Satoro

As we've seen, there's not much point in spending time worrying about what's going to happen once you quit. All worry is like to riding a stationary bike: it gives you something to do but you never get anywhere. Worrying is using your imagination in all the wrong ways. At the end of the day, what will be, will be!

Most people lower their expectations to meet their level of performance. They do this because they really don't like getting outside of their comfort zones. But outside of your comfort zone is the only place where you can make the changes you need to make in order to alter your life for the better.

Before you can successfully quit drinking, you first need to elevate your expectations about yourself and your life. Then raise your performance to meet those good expectations.

How Do You Raise Your Good Expectations?

One way of raising your expectations is by using your imagination for your benefit, otherwise known as visualization. What I mean by visualization has nothing to do with mysticism, voodoo, or any of that rubbish. Visualization is something we do all the time. Other words we use for describing the same process include imagining, dreaming up, picturing, creating, anticipating, bringing to mind, getting the picture, perceiving, worrying, fretting, puzzling, apprehending, foreboding, troubling, or just thinking. And there are many more!

When you book a vacation and think about what it's going to be like, that's a form of visualization. It's the same as when you see yourself in the new car you're going to buy, running through the route you're going to take to the airport, or just thinking about putting the kettle on.

At the opposite end of the scale is worry. Worrying is visualizing all the things that might go wrong or could go wrong. You imagine worst case scenarios of catastrophic failure. You see impending disasters. You forecast a bad year, a pitiful return, a detrimental outcome.

Seeing Before Doing

"By believing passionately in something that still does not exist, we create it. The non-existent is whatever we have not yet sufficiently desired, whatever we have not irrigated with our blood to such a degree that it becomes strong enough to stride across the somber threshold of nonexistence."

I love this quote from Nikos Kazantzakis. It illustrates clearly that thought precedes reality. If we want good things to happen, we have to envision the outcome first, then act to make those thoughts become a reality.

Many people dismiss the idea that you can affect your life with positive imagination. What you imagine can affect you not just physically, but emotionally. Just pick up any good book and you'll feel this in action for yourself. Watch any good horror, comedy, or action movie to feel the transfer of someone else's imagination into your mind, a transfer that ultimately changes how you feel or think. As the hero of the movie chases down the bad guy, your pulse will elevate along with the action. Your body and emotions react to what's going on in the plot as if you were actively taking part.

Beware the Voodoo

One caveat about visualization before we continue, you cannot make something come into existence just through the power of visualization. There are many charlatans who'll try to convince you that all you have to do is see what you want in your mind and it will magically appear, presented to you by the universe. So, if you want a sports car, just close your eyes, think hard and long, until one day you open your front door and there it is.

I'm an open minded man, so I can't dismiss something like this out of hand. But I do have my doubts. I tend to believe it from the perspective that if you keep thinking about something that you want (or don't want) in your life, it is more likely to manifest itself than if you don't ever think about it. But just thinking about it is not going to make what you desire suddenly appear. The trick is in following the thought with an action or a series of actions.

Mentally Rehearsing Your New Life

Visualization is simple: imagine yourself in the situation you would like to be in. It's a form of mental rehearsal. Build a positive mental picture of what your life will be like without alcohol. Create the belief that you can quit, that your life is going to be full, and your future will be so much better than the life you're leaving behind. Create the inner dialog that supports your belief. Seek out the thoughts and behavior that will bring you closer to making that belief your reality.

How do you visualize for your success?

Let's look at a possible future visualization about your drinking self a year down the road.

Imagine a year into your future. You are at a celebration, say a birthday party. Around you are familiar faces. Everyone is smiling and enjoying themselves. As you look at each person, notice what they're drinking. Each person has a different drink in their hands. Some people are holding cans or bottles of beer, others holding glasses of wine. Some people are drinking soft drinks or water. Now look down at your own hands. You're holding a glass of water or fruit juice. Lift the glass to your lips and take a sip. Notice how cool it is on your lips and tongue. Notice how refreshing it tastes as you swallow the water. Someone proposes a toast. See them lifting a glass of orange juice in front of them in the traditional toast. Hear them speaking the toast, raising the glass to the health of the person whose birthday it is. Raise your glass of water. How does that feel? Imagine it feeling good lifting your glass of healthy water in celebration of someone's health.

Whenever I raise a glass of water in this way, there is an added level of personal meaning for me. I am still included in the celebration and the ritual of the toast. But I feel much better about wishing for good health without poisoning myself with the traditional glass of toxic chemicals.

Reinvent Yourself by Reframing Your Life

Everything that happens to us occurs within a certain personal mental framework. Your perceptions of reality are different from mine, from the members of your family, your close friends, or anyone else. Think about a frame as your personal window through which you view the world around you. This frame is constructed from every experience that you've ever had, everything you've seen, heard, felt, smelt, tasted, or thought. As you can see, no two people could possibly see the same thing in the same way.

You have a choice about how you view things because you can change the frame. This is known as reframing.

Let's say that you've quit drinking alcohol on Monday, have gotten through the whole week, and now it's the weekend. It's Saturday evening and you've flown through your first few days. You've worked hard all week, avoided the pub, gone for a quick walk around the block in the evening as soon as you felt a craving. Your motivation has been strong up until now. You've taken a lot of strength from the early momentum and visualizations, but now you're starting to run out of steam.

This is the first Saturday you've spent without drinking alcohol. You've been doing the things you'd normally be doing every Saturday. Now is the time when you would typically be gearing yourself up for the pub. Today, you've made up your mind to stay in the house and watch a good movie with your family. As the afternoon wears on, you're feeling tired, and all you want to do is relax. A normal relaxing Saturday, for as many years back as you can remember, has meant meeting up with your friends and drinking a few pints, maybe playing a game or two of pool or darts. You start to feel like you're being cheated out of your reward for working hard all week. The drink cravings start to come on thick and fast. You start thinking - "That's it, I can't do this anymore, I'm fed up with it. These cravings are too strong and I just want to go to the pub to be with my mates".

Willpower is one thing, but you only have a certain amount to play with. Most of your willpower has been used up earlier in the day with getting around to those jobs that you've been putting off.

Ideas for Reframing

Let's look at how you can reframe this situation.

Reframing is looking at the situation and trying to find an alternative explanation for how you're feeling, alternative ways of interpreting the same thing.

You can tell yourself "I figured that there'd be times when I'd be triggered into my old behavior patterns, times when I would feel weak or tired. So I expected this and I just need to ride it out."

You can replace the idea of beer, wine, vodka and look at alcohol for what it really is, a toxic brown/red/white/clear liquid. Do you really want to put this poisonous sludge into your body?

You can think about how much you've been duped by Big Alcohol, by the propaganda and the health lies. How long are you going to let them shaft you?

You can think about the pub environment as a drug den, the bar owner as a drug dealer, and your drinking buddies as druggies. Is that where you want to be instead of spending a great afternoon with your family?

And as far as being cheated out of your reward goes, see yourself in short trousers, sucking your thumb, stamping your feet and wailing for mummy! I'm just saying!

What about your cravings? How can you reframe them?

The specific sensations that you're feeling don't really matter. You could be feeling anything from butterflies in your stomach, nervousness, twitching, whatever. What matters most is your interpretation of those specific feelings. What exactly are you telling yourself about them?

Your initial interpretation might be to tell yourself that your body is craving alcohol. An alternative, or reframed interpretation, is to smile and say to yourself that what you're feeling is your body abandoning the alcohol. Your defense system is breaking down the habit bit by bit and these feelings are evidence that your body is becoming healthy and drug free.

I used to think about the cravings as Gollum from *The Hobbit* and *Lord of the Rings* series. I played a movie in my mind of this sniveling pathetic creature begging me to take a drink, pretty please. But I could read his thoughts. He was sniggering at me when he thought I couldn't hear, thinking that he knew me, that I would crumble under his will. He became the parody of my bad habit and I took great pleasure in watching the evil little bastard slowly crumbling and dying.

Finally, **H**ave **O**nly **P**ositive **E**xpectations!

In the next section, I'm going to look at a type of reframing for raising your positivity and determination.

Raising Your Expectations to Meet Your Performance

"You cannot stop the waves, but you can learn to surf."
Jon Kabat-Zinn

When you quit drinking alcohol, two of the most important tools in your arsenal will be positivity and determination. We'll talk a bit later in this book about some methods and tactics that you can use to help you to keep yourself positive and determined.

For now let's focus on why you need these things.

Positivity

Positivity is about being your own best friend. Positivity, in this instance, is telling yourself that you can stop using alcohol, that you're heading into a new phase in your life and that it's time to leave your old self behind.

There's a whole branch of psychology, known as *positive psychology*, which is devoted to teaching ways to achieve a good life, rather than just treating problems or mental issues. The whole approach is based around adjusting negative thinking styles so that a person can make their own changes to how they feel, how they think, and ultimately how they live their lives.

Positivity is often seen as unrealistic, its practitioners spending their days seeing the world through impractical rose tinted glasses. Abraham Lincoln said *"Most folks are about as happy as they make up their minds to be."* Positive thinking is not about putting your head in the sand when it comes to your difficulties, or pretending that life doesn't suck sometimes. It's about dealing with difficulties as they happen, and dealing with them in the best way you know how. If you don't know how to deal with these issues, you can always learn.

Determination

When you ask people what is the one predictor of success in life, most of them would say intelligence. While having a head full of smarts does help, it's not the key factor. There are plenty of people who are just as clever as Mark Zuckerberg yet achieve no great success in life.

Determination is more valuable than intelligence because, in the face of adversity, the person with the most determination will keep pushing until the task is achieved. Again, to quote Lincoln, *"Determine that the thing can and shall be done, and then we shall find the way"*.

I'm not belittling the notion of intelligence, it can play a vital role in choosing the right path to take. No matter how determined you are, if you're continuously driving yourself down the wrong path, you'll always fail. The determined individual, using some intelligence, will not be defeated, but instead will reassess the situation, choose a different course, and keep going.

Alcohol as a Tool

Drinking alcohol has its benefits, even if those benefits are causing you pain and discomfort. Drinking can be a strategy for dealing with pain or problems, it can be a way to relax or to socialize. It's not a very good strategy, but it is a strategy nonetheless.

Quitting alcohol will cause internal and external conflicts. The problem is that, up until now, you've probably been using alcohol to help you deal with a lot of different conflicts in your life. Once you make the decision to quit, you won't have this method at your disposal any more.

The discomfort is almost inevitable. But, as we've seen, most of the discomfort is in your mind. It's a natural part of the adjusting and transitioning process that moves you from using to not using alcohol. It's as simple as that. You need to go through this discomfort to make the necessary changes to your rituals. Keep in mind that the uncomfortable feelings are just a part of the change process. They don't last long. Like any other mental process, how you think about the discomfort will go a long way in determining how strong these feelings are and how long they last. Only you can reframe the discomfort so it comes out in your favor.

Using Positivity and Determination

Positivity and determination are the fuels that will help to propel your efforts forward. You must begin this process by making the decision to stop using and stick to that decision. Make the commitment as if your life depended on it because it does. Look for ways to build your determination through the people in your life. Focus on what you want, rather than what you don't want. Kill any negative thoughts as soon as they happen. Believe in your own ability and rerun your beliefs over and over in your head as many times as necessary.

Keep it simple and stay strong.

In the next section, we'll focus on writing down your reasons to quit.

ALCOHOL FREEDOM • 30

Why? Why? Why?

"A man always has two reasons for doing anything: a good reason and the real reason."
J. P. Morgan

I could sit here for a full day writing about the reasons for you to change. Most of them would mean nothing to you because my reasons to change are different to yours. We all live our lives with our own perceptions about ourselves and the outside world. It's your perceptions about your reality that will influence your reasons to quit.

Health Reasons to Quit?

Take health reasons, for instance. Nobody really needs to explain the important health reasons to stop drinking. Does it really matter to you that about 2,500,000 million people die every year because of alcohol, more than ten times the combined death rate for all illegal drugs combined?(1)(2) Does it really matter that alcohol is responsible for over 200 medical conditions?(3) Most people who consider quitting are thinking about it partly because of the possible consequences to their health. Even people who don't see any reason to quit will know about some of the health risks, even if they don't see these risks applying to them.

If you're at the stage where you're contemplating walking away from alcohol, you're certainly feeling some negative consequences in your body, in your relationships, or in some other area of your life. Just knowing about these negative consequences is normally enough to force you to at least start thinking about what you're doing. But it's never going to be enough to convince you to quit if you don't *want* to quit.

Do You Really Want This?

Thinking that you want to quit is not the same as actually quitting. Many people feel they need to quit because they're afraid of the consequences if they don't. They don't like spending so much money on the booze. They don't like the impression they're portraying of themselves while they're drunk. They might be getting a lot of grief from their spouse or from their parents or friends. Maybe they've overslept one morning too many and their boss has made it clear that this is their last chance. All these are legitimate reasons to stop using alcohol, but are they enough for you?

If you don't really want to quit using alcohol, if deep down you believe that alcohol still has a part to play in your life, you'll find steering clear of alcohol very difficult in the long run. In the beginning, it's very easy to find and build momentum, to psyche yourself up enough and push through the first few days and weeks. But if you don't have that self-determination, the early momentum that gave you such a boost will fade rapidly. All the conflicts that provided you with your reasons to quit won't seem as urgent. As a result, the temptation of alcohol will return with a passion.

To overcome this, you need to sit down and think about your personal reasons to quit.

Internal or External?

First, think about where your reasons to quit are really coming from. Are they internal or external? Are they your reasons or are they being forced on you by someone else? If they are not yours, you need to figure out how to make them yours.

Let's clarify internal versus external.

An external reason to quit is something that's motivating you from the outside. It could be your wife, your boss, or your kids expressing their concern about your drinking. You might have been stopped by the police for drunk driving, or you may have said something you didn't mean or don't remember saying, done something really stupid, and so on.

An internal reason to quit is something which is motivating you from the inside. It might very well be influenced by something or someone outside of you, but the main force of the motivation is internal. It could be a physical feeling, pain, discomfort, and so on. An example might be your hangovers hitting you harder or lasting longer. Or maybe you are beginning to feel pain in your liver area. There are also internal psychological motivations. You might feel that your life is wasting away or that you are a bad influence on your kids. You could be worried about your liver and other organs, fearing the level of damage that you've done after so many years of alcohol use.

Any reason to quit can be the logic behind the decision. Why are you taking a certain direction? Why are you quitting? What's in it for you? What's in it for the people you care about? The logic behind your decision has to be persuasive enough to keep you on track during tough times or through any periods of self-doubt.

Internal reasons to quit can have very a different motivational impact than external reasons.

External Motivation

Let's take another look at an external motivation. Say your wife is telling you that she thinks you're drinking too much or she doesn't like the state you're getting yourself into while you're drunk. She's fearful about your health, about the message you're sending to the kids, and she really wants you to stop. This is certainly a motivating force, no doubt about it. Obviously you don't want to upset your spouse. You can see she's genuinely concerned, so you tell her that you will try to stop. However, if you're not on the same page as her, if you think your drinking is not as bad as she thinks it is, how motivating is that going to be for you in the long run?

I've had plenty of people coming up to me the day after a heavy night of alcohol use, telling me I'd been a bit too drunk, that I'd said or done something stupid, or telling me that they were worried about what I was doing to my health. My dad was forever advising me to watch my liver. I always brushed it off. I might have thought a little about the physical consequences of my alcohol use, but at the end of the day I'd think, "I'm a big boy and I know what I'm doing". In reality, I didn't want anything to get in the way or spoil the 'fun'.

The problem with using an external motivation to stop drinking is you can always pass the buck when things are not going well. Change is always accompanied by discomfort. As soon as you feel the first signs of being uncomfortable, it's going to be much easier to tell yourself that this wasn't your decision. You can tell yourself you were forced into it, emotionally blackmailed, or pressured, that you really didn't want to quit in the first place. Once you feel the inevitable discomfort of the actual quit, it won't take much of a stretch for you to start rethinking your choices and backtracking to an alternative strategy. Then, you'll convince yourself it's not really your drinking that's at fault, it's the *amount* that you're drinking. All you need to do is to have more control. You can carry on doing what you're doing, but you just need to cut down. Handy!

When you drink to get drunk, moderation is, at best, a short-term strategy. It's only a matter of time before your consumption starts to expand again.

Internal Motivation

Internal motivations, on the other hand, are far more compelling. If your reason to quit is because you have a pain in your liver, for instance, it could be a life-or-death situation for you. Even the thought of cirrhosis of the liver is enough to panic most people. An internal motivation is a *complete change of thinking*. You learn something new, you change your perceptions, or you get a 'wake-up call'. Whatever it is, you've learned something which has changed the way you think and should change the way you behave, forever.

With internal motivations, you cannot pass the buck. The buck stops right here with you! An internal motivation will follow you everywhere you go. You have nowhere to hide. You can always get drunk to temporarily evade this new way of thinking or this knowledge, but underneath every drink you take, there'll be a deep sadness or frustration or contempt or disgust about what you're doing. That type of incentive to change is very, very powerful. It forces you to confront yourself like no external reason to quit can ever get close to.

One of the most powerful internal motivations for me was when I faced up to the fact that my alcohol use had fostered and influenced the same behavior in my son. Most of us are unaware or unwilling to face the fact that alcohol is a drug or that we are drug users. In terms of overall harms, alcohol is more harmful than heroin. Once you recognize this fact, you can't escape the knowledge. It alters your perception.

As a parent, when I first switched on to this perception, it was a hard truth to take. The psychological and physical pain I felt at that time was intense. Even thinking about it now, two years later, is enough to stir uncomfortable images in my mind.

Goal-Oriented Internal Motivation

Another powerful internal motivational force, and reason to quit, is learning new things and beginning new challenges, while setting yourself new goals. This type of motivation can be very helpful in overcoming any bad habits because the thinking and behaviors that result from pursuing these new goals can act like a self-fulfilling prophecy. You begin with the thought. You analyze what it is that you want to do, what would bring you pleasure and joy, fulfillment and happiness, self-control and self-belief. These thoughts lead to actions. When you have focused and desirable actions, they drive your performance. This performance reinforces the behavior, which feeds the good thinking, which leads to more action, better performance, more good thinking, and on and on. You create your own cycle of motivation.

Who Are Your Reasons To Quit?

So, how do you find your strongest internal motivations? Well, that's up to you. Your set of motivations is unique to you. But we all find our motivations in roughly the same places: the people, places, things, and goals in our lives.

What drives you?

Think about your life as it stands right now. Who are the most important people in your life? What are the most important things to you right now? What do you want to do in your life? What would bring you the greatest amount of self-esteem, joy, and fulfilment?

Spend some time writing down your reasons for using alcohol and your reasons for not using, a list of the pros and cons of your alcohol use, if you like. Take a sheet of paper and draw a line straight down the middle. On the right-hand side, make a list of every reason you have for continuing to use alcohol, the pros. On the left-hand side, make a list of every reason you have for not drinking anymore, the cons.

Now, look at each item on your list and see how they affect those people that you care about.

Next, think about your general obstacles. You can use a separate sheet of paper for this. Write down the obstacles that might get in the way of you achieving your goals. Where do you think you'll crave a drink the most? When? With who? What routines or rituals can you identify that instigate or propel you to drink? Who are the people you can turn to for support? Who should you avoid?

Next, let's take a look at planning for your first day of freedom.

(1) http://www.who.int/substance_abuse/publications/global_alcohol_report/msbgsruprofiles.pdf (Page 32)
(2)   http://www.drugfree.org/join-together/drug-abuse-kills-200000-people-each-year-un-report/
(3) http://www.who.int/mediacentre/factsheets/fs349/en/

The Power of Locking Down Your Alcohol Quit Day

"Be Prepared... the meaning of the motto is that a scout must prepare himself by previous thinking out and practicing how to act on any accident or emergency so that he is never taken by surprise."
Robert Baden-Powell

When it comes to picking a date to finish drinking alcohol, don't choose tomorrow. It can sometimes make a lot of sense to grab the bull by the horns and just to go for it. But there's a very good reason for not rushing into this. You need the time to make an effective plan about how you're going to deal with any difficulties. You also need the time to get your head and environment into the right place.

By making an effective plan, I don't mean you have to construct an intricate moment -by-moment timetable about how you're going to get through each day, what you're going to do in this or that situation, or how you'll respond to every jerk who offers you a drink. You can certainly make life much easier on yourself by a little forward thinking and preparation.

You should have at least a few good strategies in place for helping you to avoid or get you through some of the more difficult situations. There are also some useful techniques that you can use for redirecting and reprogramming your habitual brain. We'll delve a bit more into that later.

Why Does Setting a Date Work?

Let's get back to locking down your alcohol quit day.

The reason why setting a date works so well is that it cements your decision into a specific time frame and gives you a definite target to aim towards. Both of these things are important elements for keeping everything under your control. Without setting a date, it gets too easy to put things off. It's too easy to say, "I'll do it next week!" or, "It's just not a good time right now" or, "I'll quit once this (or that) is out of the way". We all know that tomorrow never comes and that there is never going to be a perfect situation.

By locking down your alcohol quit day, you also give yourself the time to get your affairs in order. This is very important. You should be starting your new journey with as little pressure as possible.

Telling Your Family

Setting a specific date in the near future allows you to sort out who you *want* to tell, and who you *need* to tell. Giving the people who matter in your life some advanced warning is essential for a number of reasons. The most important reason is to give your family the chance of digesting how your decision is going to impact their lives.

When you decide to quit drinking, it's a choice that not only affects you; it affects everyone who is close to you. And the closer they are, the more they are going to be affected.

We'll talk more about telling your family in a later chapter.

Choosing Your Quit Date

Choose a date within a reasonable timespan.

There's always a danger in over-thinking things when you give yourself too much time. Setting a date focuses your mind into a specific time frame. I'd recommend that you set your date between one and two weeks in advance, and certainly no more than four.

Choose a date without any built-in problems.

Your priority in the first couple of days is to stay calm, relaxed, and away from alcohol. So don't choose a day when you would otherwise be celebrating, when your mind would normally expect you to be drinking alcohol. You'll learn how to deal with days like these as you make progress. Celebration is a healthy part of life but putting yourself into a situation where everyone is getting drunk while you're on your alcohol quit day is asking for trouble.

The first days should be made as easy as possible. Try to engineer things so you have few distractions. Make sure everyone else is on the same page as you. Everything should revolve around you and your transformation, that is the number one priority, so don't let anyone or anything get in the way.

Choose a date with personal significance.

You could choose one of the many days that holds a relatively important cultural or personal significance in your life. New Year's Day is the first one that springs to mind. Another is your birthday. Ordinarily, you've probably used your birthday as an excuse for a giant piss-up. This is the beginning of your personal New Year. You're a year older and a lot wiser. You're going to spend the rest of your birthdays poison-free, so why not start now?

Reminders

Buy a big calendar and circle your starting date with a big red marker to make it stand out. Now put the calendar in a place where everyone can see it, like on the fridge door, the kitchen cupboard, or above the TV. This will act as a constant reminder. It's also a big part of publicizing your commitment to yourself and to the important people in your life. Something else you can do is to write the date on sticky notes and plaster them all over your home in prominent places.

Other Reasons

Another reason for taking the time to plan your quit date is so you can go to your doctor, which we'll look at in the next section. If you are a woman who suffers from PMS, you may want to choose your timing carefully to avoid your period.

Without your brain being bathed in this poisonous solvent you'll become a much more capable individual. In the short term, it's all about getting used to not having alcohol as part of your life any more. These first few days are often a challenge to everyone who goes through them. By spending some advance time in planning and preparation, you'll be making the start day and the days that follow as easy and relaxed as possible. Life is full of challenges and discomfort, as we all know. All we can do is to deal with each challenge as it happens.

Next, should you get advice from your doctor?

Should You See Your Doctor Before You Quit?

"Precaution is better than cure."
Johann Wolfgang von Goethe

I didn't see my doctor when I quit. The reason is partly because my partner Esther and I had only moved to Spain the year before and I hadn't yet got around to signing up with a doctor. Also, I knew that I could quit without any serious side effects because I'd stopped drinking for almost a year in 2009 without any ill effects. Over the next five years, I had spells of one or two days without drinking, sometimes longer. So I knew that if my health wasn't taking a plunge after a couple of days off the drink, I was unlikely to suffer from any short-term complications. Above all, I didn't go to the doctor because not going to the doctor was my choice to make, as was quitting alcohol.

Having said that, I'm not suggesting that you shouldn't pay a precautionary visit to your own doctor. I'm not a doctor, I don't have any practical medical training, and I'm not in any position to give you advice about your health or about the specific side effects that you might encounter when you stop drinking. To be on the safe side, consult with your doctor or get some other medical advice specific to your own situation before you stop drinking.

What Can Your Doctor Tell You?

What should you expect from your seeing your doctor?

Don't expect your doctor to be able to prescribe a magic elixir that will completely and permanently take away your bad habit. That's not going to happen. Apart from offering you medication, your doctor should be able to offer you a sympathetic ear and some relevant advice.

Your doctor is probably the person who's in the best position to evaluate your risk because she knows you and your medical background. You must be open and honest about your alcohol use if you expect your doctor to be able to give you the correct and useful advice. If you sit in front of your doctor and censor the information you're handing to her, you're just wasting your time and hers.

If you drink two bottles of wine a day but you tell your doctor you're only drinking two glasses a day, how is she supposed to evaluate your risk? If you drink two bottles of wine a day, then state that you drink two bottles of wine a day. Above all, your doctor is there to help you, so never withhold crucial information.

Everything you tell your doctor should be confidential, so you shouldn't have to worry about anyone else finding out. On the other hand, you don't have to treat your visit like you're in the confessional. Never feel obliged to divulge the non-medical personal parts life if you don't want to.

Your doctor will also make a determination about the amount of likely damage that's already been caused. She might take blood samples for liver enzyme tests, which can help diagnose liver damage. She can also arrange for consultations with specialists if she suspects any underlying damage. She may also recommend places where you can go for help.

What Can't Your Doctor Tell You?

If you're asking your doctor for information about your future symptoms, all she can do is give you a very general idea. She'll give you the same general list of common symptoms and side effects that you can find on any medical website. Most doctors don't use a crystal ball. They can only give you a rough prediction as to how long the symptoms will last, how you'll feel, if you'll lose sleep, get the shakes, or have hallucinations with little green men, and so on.

In the next section, we'll look at minimizing the predictable roadblocks that might come your way.

Alcohol Freedom Mindset Two

Your Behavior Triggers are at the Root of Your Alcohol Cravings

"Our subconscious minds have no sense of humor, play no jokes and cannot tell the difference between reality and an imagined thought or image. What we continually think about eventually will manifest in our lives."
Robert Collier

What Are Triggers?

A habit sequence consists of three parts. First is the trigger, then the behavior, and finally the reward. Triggers act like switches in your mind or in your environment. They are the unconscious sparks that launch the behavior part of your habit sequence. In this case the behavior is to drink alcohol. Taking the action leads you to your reward, which we'll look at in more detail later. Triggers are the backbone of your cravings. They are the spark that keeps firing off, persistently pushing you towards taking the action.

One of the goals in clearing out unwanted habits is to bring the normally subconscious patterns of thought into your conscious awareness. You can't change anything if it's happening without you even knowing that it's happening. So before you can change the behavior, you need to know and understand the unconscious triggers. Once you know your triggers, you can deliberately alter the flow of the habit by inserting a diversion between the trigger and the drinking. I'll get into these diversions a little later.

Are Triggers Bad?

Triggers are neither good nor bad, they're just part of how we humans think and act. They're the links in the chain that lead us from one automatic action to another.

Let's take some simple examples. When you wake up in the morning, your bladder sends a "full" signal to your brain which triggers the desire to use the toilet.

Walking into the kitchen triggers you to automatically switch on the kettle or the coffee machine.

As you pass by the bakery on your way to work, the smell of fresh bread triggers your mouth to water, your stomach to groan, and a desire to sink your teeth into a soft warm bagel.

Seeing a jogger on your way home from work, triggers you to think about the few extra pounds you've put on over the holiday season.

The Sophisticated Mind

Most triggers fire off without you being aware of them. As you drive to work in the morning, you don't have to consciously think about every movement, every gear change, and every brake press. Your mind could be a million miles away from what's happening in front on you. You might be consciously thinking about how badly your team played in last night's league game, or how you think the conversation should be managed in this morning's staff meeting, or how you can deal with that stupid dog who keeps pissing all over the carpet. As these thoughts are occurring, your body is cocooned inside a chunk of metal that's hurtling down the road at 60 miles an hour or winding through the busy rush hour city traffic.

This level of sophisticated thinking can only be achieved because your mind has relegated much of the driving to the subconscious. It is these habit chains of trigger-action-reward that are keeping you alive as you speed down the highway. Your habit brain is automatically triggering adjustments to how fast you're going, pressing the accelerator to speed up or touching the break to slow down. By turning the steering wheel slightly to the left or to the right, you keep the car between the white lines to avoid smacking into the cars on either side of you. You don't have to 'think' about any of these movements. They just happen automatically.

From the time you get up in the morning until the time you fall asleep at night, you're influenced by thousands of these programmed switches, clicking away behind the scenes, influencing every action you take.

Routine and Ambush Triggers

As you become aware of your alcohol triggers, you'll find that there are two types, I call them routine triggers and ambush triggers.

Routine triggers are linked to any action that you do every day. Some examples of routine alcohol triggers include finishing work, coming home, passing the pub, or eating your evening meal.

Routine triggers tend to activate at the same times, in the same places, and often with the same people. Heavy drinkers are surrounded by this type of trigger. You might have a *finished work for the day* alcohol trigger as you pack away your tools for the day. As you leave work, a *pass by the pub* trigger fires off in your brain, flooding your mind with images of your favorite drink.

As you walk up to your local bar you'll have countless triggers firing off. You might have a *pub door* trigger where just seeing the familiar bar door gets your mouth watering. As you open the door and walk into the pub, the *pub smell* trigger and *pub sound* trigger welcomes you as a matter of course. Then you get the *see bar counter and beer taps* trigger, the *favorite barstool* trigger, the *familiar faces* trigger - and so on.

This type of trigger tends to blend seamlessly into your daily routine. One trigger leads to another, and before you know it four or five hours have passed and you're onto your twelfth drink.

The second type of trigger, the ambush trigger, is always unexpected and unpredictable. Ambush triggers account for all those times when a drinking buddy has called you on the phone out of the blue asking if you're gonna come out for a few beers. They fire off when you hear some bad news and you feel the need to commiserate with yourself. They fire off when you hear good news and you want to celebrate. Even though these ambush triggers are beyond your control when they happen, they can still be managed.

As we've seen, triggers are neither good nor bad. They're an essential part of any automatic behavior. In the next few sections, we're going to take a look at the types of triggers that influence your alcohol use. We'll also take a look at how you can isolate and easily modify your triggers.

How to Discover and Crush Your Alcohol Triggers

"Your pain is the breaking of the shell that encloses your understanding."
Khalil Gibran

Now that you know what triggers are, it's time to find out which triggers are firing off in your brain, the ones that are causing you to crave your next drink.

Everyone has a different sequence of triggers. I could hand you a long list of triggers that used to fire off my alcohol-drinking urges, but you will only recognize a few of them in your own behavior. Your own triggers are the things, places, times, and people in your life that make you think about using alcohol. They are part of your thoughts, emotions, and self-talk.

Finding Your Triggers?

How do you find your triggers? One of the simplest methods of uncovering your triggers is to take out a sheet of paper and make a list. Don't worry at this stage about finding every one of them. Even if you know your triggers pretty well, there are some you're bound to exclude.

Writing down your list of triggers serves a few different functions. First, it gets you to think about your individual triggering processes. What exactly is happening in your mind that sparks off the action of taking that first drink?

Taking the first sip is the end result of a sequence of thoughts. To find your triggers, you need to work your way backwards through your thought processes to the thoughts or actions that are triggering the whole sequence.

Tracing Your Triggers

Writing your thoughts gives you a step-by-step backwards glance at what's going on, which ultimately brings your alcohol use triggers into your conscious awareness and focus. This is the only place where you can deal with your triggers.

Half the battle in overcoming any unwanted habit is to know and understand the events and sequences of that habit. The basic idea is that once you can understand this chain of thoughts and actions, you'll start to become aware of the weak spots where you can inject your awareness, and ultimately divert your thought flow away from your alcohol use and towards healthier behaviors.

Some triggers are not as obvious as others and can take a lot more digging around to uncover. As you write down your most obvious triggers, the writing process will naturally uncover some of the not-so-obvious triggers.

Interrupting the Flow

Once you have a list of your triggers, you can begin to work through them one by one. As you examine each habit sequence, look for the most obvious areas where you can interrupt the flow. The idea is to find the place in the sequence where you can introduce an alternative thought or action which will either kill the urge or lead to a behavior other than drinking alcohol.

Triggering Thirst

Like many people, a usual time for me to start using alcohol was in the evening, once I'd finished work. I'd pack all the tools in the back of my Land Rover and drive into town to get to that first creamy pint. Going from work to the pub just felt like a completely natural part of my day. It was something that I'd always done, right from the first time I got paid, and something I'd seen other people doing all my life. Even thinking back to when I was a child, I remember watching the steady stream of men in their work clothes filing through the pub doors once clocking off time came around.

When I started to examine my behavior, after I had quit using alcohol, I realized that the urges I felt at the end of the working day were the culmination of a powerful triggering sequence that kicked off around lunchtime and gradually built up during the afternoon. The intensity of this build-up was so strong that by the time I'd finished work, I was absolutely gagging for a drink.

I had assumed that it was just finishing work that was sparking off my thirst. The day was over, I'd finished my work, and the clock was telling me it was time for a pint. Furthermore, I always thought I deserved the after-work trip to the pub. It was my reward for working hard.

Snowballing Dehydration

In fact, once I started to think about it, I realized that the after-work triggers to drink began sparking off around lunch time.

When I took my lunch break, sitting in the van with a pack of sandwiches, I might start to think about what time we'd finish. Then I'd get the first fleeting images of sitting on my regular bar stool in the corner of my local bar. I might think about one of my drinking buddies, or how nice the pint would taste, smell, or look. Once that thinking process started, it would build as the afternoon wore on.

As my thoughts manufactured the anticipation, I'd actually stop drinking water. I was subconsciously dehydrating myself so that by the time I finished work I was absolutely parched. My mouth and lips would be bone dry, I'd be thirsty, tired, and irritable. By the end of the day, my body would be screaming for a drink and my thoughts would only be on quenching the thirst as soon as possible.

My mind would translate those thoughts into "I can't wait for a pint - I'm gagging".

Once I got into the pub, the pints cured any signs of dehydration. Of course my mind was telling me a different story. Here I was on my favorite stool in my corner of my bar. I was relaxed, happy, finished work, not tired any more, friends around me, warm, dry, and at peace with all mankind. In reality, every time I quenched this forced dehydration trigger with those first few pints, the behavior was positively reinforced. The pattern became easier and easier to follow, until it finally became a ritual.

Look at your own drinking from this perspective. Can you see how your behaviors are easily reinforced until they become habits?

Same Trigger, Multiple Triggering

So thinking about what was really happening when I finished work, and tracing the sequence backwards, I realized that most of my cravings for alcohol turned out to be nothing more than good old thirst. Once I understood what was going on, it was simple to prevent the sequence from playing out by constantly checking how much water I was drinking, especially in the late afternoon. I'd make sure to drink a cup of water every time I stopped to fill the chainsaw with petrol, which was about every 20 to 30 minutes.

This didn't completely eliminate the desire to go to the pub when I finished work because the dehydration was only one of my alcohol-drinking triggers. But it highlighted other areas of my life where the thirst trigger was also playing a prominent role. By knowing that the trigger existed, it was easier to cancel it out.

As I've illustrated, everyone will experience different triggers, but there are a few common areas where we can concentrate our attention. These are places, times, people, and your emotions. We'll look at each of these over the following pages.

Alcohol Freedom Mindset Three

Engineer Your Optimal Quit Drinking Environment

"You can't make positive choices for the rest of your life without an environment that makes those choices easy, natural, and enjoyable."
Deepak Chopra

The User-Mentality Prison

It's very difficult to deal with any problems in life if we're still in the same state of mind that we were when we created them. When you quit drinking alcohol, your mind is still going to be firmly locked into that user-mentality prison.

It's a lot easier to think about the immediate and certain gratification or relief you are going to get from drinking the alcohol in this moment than some far off and uncertain pain that might be the result of taking that drink. When difficulties arise, your first thought could very well be using alcohol, heading to the nearest bar, or taking a quick spin down to the local supermarket for a few hours of relief.

The first few days and weeks of your quit are about becoming aware of and ultimately ambushing those automatic alcohol-drinking thoughts. These thoughts are an unwanted part of your old habit and old programming that needs to be weeded out and destroyed. Breaking that programming involves separating the cause from the effect. This means taking apart the sequence of events from the trigger to the reward, removing the unwanted parts, and replacing them with more favorable alternatives.

With your old drinking sequence, every time you got stressed or upset about a problem, your automatic reaction was to first think about drinking, then to have a drink, and finally to get drunk.

You may use the excuse that you deserve a drink as a reward for all your efforts during the day. When you come home from work, you grab a beer from the fridge or a glass of wine, sit in your favorite chair, take a drink, and relax.

As I've discussed in the previous chapter about triggering, this is a sequence of events that most often happens without any need for your conscious awareness. This is not something that's happened overnight. These automatic reactions have imperceptibly grown into your habit over many years. Drinking alcohol has become a part of who you are, a part of your routine, a part of your day, and a part of your environment.

We'll take a longer look at some of the more common triggers in a later chapter and what you can do to break the associations between trigger and action. For now, let's concentrate on how your environment influences your alcohol use and what you can do about it.

There are three general ways to use your environment to help you quit drinking. You can change your environment, change aspects of your environment, or change your perceptions about your environment.

Changing Your Environment

Changing your environment means completely removing yourself from your current place and going somewhere else. A permanent change from the environment that encourages your alcohol use is the most preferable option. If you move to a country where alcohol is banned, for instance, you solve your problem immediately. If you can't get alcohol, you can't drink it. This tactic will most likely also involve a complete cultural change. This is not something that most of us would be willing or able to do.

An alternative method of achieving the same results, at least for your first couple of weeks, is to use your vacation time to get away from the usual stresses and strains of your familiar life. Thinking about using your vacation in this way can be a bit of a jolt for most people because we usually look at our vacation as the time when we get to do what we want without worrying about the consequences. If you're a heavy alcohol user, vacation times usually involves lots of unbridled alcohol use. On vacation, we get to throw out all the old conventions about not drinking every day, or even not drinking before a certain time in the day. When we're on holiday, we're entitled to do whatever we want.

If you think about it, what other time in your life will you get the opportunity to remove all the daily alcohol reminders in one fell swoop? When else do you get the chance to leave behind the normal stresses and strains of daily living?

Think about all the vacations you've taken in the past. These are the times of the year when you're supposed to be recuperating, recharging your batteries, and returning to your normal life with renewed energy and focus. This energy and focus has got to last you for the next four to six months, or maybe even for a full year; at least until your next vacation comes round. Instead, we use our vacation time to overindulge in food and alcohol. By the time we get home, and we are once again facing our regular routine, we're even more tired than when we started. We almost need another vacation. Something is very wrong with this picture!

My First Proper Vacation

I took the first vacation of my new alcohol-free life, late 2013. We drove to the South of Spain to a small Andalusian village called Competa. Competa is a white-washed village overlooking the southern Mediterranean Sea, about an hour's drive from Málaga.

Before I went, I was very concerned about what I was going to do once I got there. I would have actually preferred to stay at home and carry on working on my website. It turned out to be an amazing experience. It was the first time I got into the holiday spirit without trying to fill every waking hour with drinking alcohol or thinking about drinking alcohol.

Every vacation I had ever taken before was filled with booze and food. I knew I wasn't going to do much else, so I didn't plan to do anything else. By the end of each holiday, I never had any real memories. I only had this mush of images that involved food and copious amounts of alcohol, drunkenness, and hangovers. If I'd visited a beautiful place like Competa in the past, it would have been totally wasted because of my drinking.

Now that I was taking a vacation as a non-drinker, I was compelled to think about what I was going to do to pass the time. But I had no experience to draw on apart from drinking. What do you actually do on a holiday? I had no idea! This was all very new for me. So I planned to visit the local town, drive to some of the nearby towns, go to the beach, and to walk a lot. It ended up being amazing. It was a real eye opener. This was what I'd been missing all along. Instead of nursing a daily hangover that just got deeper as the holiday progressed, I got up every morning raring to go. Considering we only went for a few days, we really packed in a lot.

The best thing is that I can remember so much from that holiday, even after a year and a half. It was also the first time I ever came back from a holiday feeling like I'd taken a break, feeling fully recharged and stoked about getting back to work.

Changing Aspects of Your Environment

If you can't change your entire environment for a few weeks, changing aspects of your environment is the next best thing. This involves shaping your environment so that it blends with your new thinking. Essentially, you'll be getting rid of any alcohol reminders. You'll also be adding things to your environment to aid your progress. We'll talk more about altering your environment later in this section.

Changing Your Perceptions about Your Environment

Changing your perceptions about your environment is the most difficult part of this process. This is because altering your perceptions involves bringing the subconscious, automatic, cause-and-effect thinking, into your conscious awareness. You have to think clearly about what you're doing or what you're about to do and adjust your thoughts as you make progress. This type of thinking takes time to master.

These changes are much easier to implement as time passes. Once you get used to not using alcohol, the reprogramming becomes almost automatic. But in the first few days, it takes a lot of conscious effort to constantly bring your mind towards what you're trying to achieve and away from thinking about alcohol.

Next, we're going to look at some of the ways you can change your immediate environment.

Creating Your Personal Coping Stronghold

"Problems are not the problem; coping is the problem."
Virginia Satir

Willpower is something you need to a certain extent when you stop drinking alcohol. We all have willpower that we can call on. If we didn't, we wouldn't be able to curtail the slightest urge. We think about willpower as being something we use when we want to bring the full force of our mighty brain to the task of doing or not doing something. We use willpower as an override for our natural inclinations, or more specifically as a way of deflecting our automatic behaviors.

The problem with willpower is that we only have it in a limited supply. For most of us, our stores of willpower are all but depleted by the time we arrive home at the end of the day.

Is Willpower Essential?

The question is, do you really need to use your willpower every time you want to stay away from alcohol? Think about all the times in your life when you didn't use alcohol because you just couldn't drink it. For instance, if you have to drive and you don't want to run the risk of getting a DUI, you won't take any alcohol. Or you won't drink if you need to make a good impression on someone, for example if you're going out on a first date. Likewise, looking like a complete piss-head in front of the big boss is not an option, so you choose to stay sober. These are all examples of times, when for one reason or another, we just can't drink, period.

During those times, we accept that we can't drink. We don't make a big deal out of it. We just get along with what needs to be done. We might think about how much we would love to sink a really cool pint at that moment, or how we could murder a glass of Chardonnay, but we don't get all hot and bothered about it. Nor do we suffer through massive withdrawal symptoms and cravings. This is because our environment is not supporting our alcohol use right then and there. When you absolutely can't have a drink, you don't need willpower. You just don't drink.

Manufacturing Your Quit-Alcohol Environment

You can use this knowledge in your first few days by deliberately manufacturing that type of environment, one that won't support your alcohol-drinking.

The secret to quitting drinking forever is not putting the alcohol into your mouth - forever. For most people, that's a daunting prospect. People don't like the idea of forever, especially the idea of not doing something that they believe they are enjoying forever. Luckily we don't live our lives that way. We live our lives moment by moment. So you don't have to deal with forever, but only with this present moment.

Your Coping Stronghold

Most cravings, temptations, urges, or whatever you want to call them, have a limited time span. They are momentary thoughts in your mind that may or may not trigger feelings in your body. As we've seen in the previous chapter, these cravings, temptations, or urges are most likely triggered by something or someone in your environment. These triggers fire off alcohol-related thoughts which then cause the feelings or emotions in your body that we label as cravings, urges, or temptations.

By reducing the incidence of alcohol triggers in your environment, you reduce or eliminate your cravings. You can't be triggered to drink alcohol if there are no triggers to spark you off.

By removing the obvious triggers from your immediate environment, particularly in your home, you're creating a controlled coping stronghold. This coping stronghold lets you have a zone where you can relax while you deal with your psychological triggers.

When you're trying to quit drinking, if every time you open your fridge, you're confronted by bottles of your favorite beer, your willpower is going to take a battering. The more hits your willpower takes, the more depleted it's going to get. It's much more sensible to stock your fridge with chilled water.

It's also important to set yourself up with little victories in the beginning. By having this coping stonghold where you can successfully avoid alcohol, you're setting yourself up with a positive string of wins before you tackle some of your more challenging environments.

Try to make your coping stonghold as free from alcohol reminders as possible. First, chuck out all alcohol. Next, get rid of the paraphernalia associated with alcohol - throw out the corkscrews, bottle openers, alcohol specific glasses, and so on. If something reminds you of drinking, throw it out, put it into a back room, or cover it up.

Next, what can you do about challenging environments in the early days of busting your habit?

Places and Situations That Activate Your Alcohol Drinking Urges and What You Can Do About Them

"All men are tempted. There is no man that lives that can't be broken down, provided it is the right temptation, put in the right spot."
Henry Ward Beecher

One of the most frequently asked questions I'm emailed at alcoholmastery.com is something like:

"Can I still go out with my mates to the pub?"

It's a nice idea, but not very practical, especially in the early days. Here are some of the problems.

Primarily you're exposing yourself to way too many temptations just by being in that environment.

As we saw in the last section, the first few days and weeks need to be as alcohol-reminder-free as possible. You don't need a massive amount of willpower to avoid a trigger that's not being sparked off. The pub is the worst place you can be. Everything is a trigger. Plus you have the added pain of your mates giving you a hard time.

Second, you'll feel like you're on the outside looking in, which puts massive pressure on you from a social perspective.

We all want to fit in with our peers and nobody wants to feel left out. If you are the only one not drinking, you're definitely going to feel like the odd one out. Everyone else is getting drunk, but you're not. This will be very boring for you. Besides, most users don't want to be in the company of non-users because you'll remember everything that goes on and they won't. This could be very embarrassing. What happens in the bar, stays in the bar, except in your case.

Third, the people you associate with all tend to share very similar interests and goals.

Ask yourself what are the common interests and goals that you share with these people now that you don't drink any more. If there's no commonality, apart from your past drinking, that relationship isn't serving any good purpose. If you have common interests that are outside of alcohol - you might play football, golf, or go fishing together - then there's no reason why you can't continue to meet with your mates outside the pub, as long as there's no pressure for you to use alcohol.

New Life, New Thinking

At the end of the day, if you want to stay alcohol free, you need to use your creativity to come up with other social activities that don't involve bars. Use your preparation time before you quit to think about what else you're going to do and do those activities from day one. Bars are for drinkers, if you want to be a non-drinker, why are you there?

Again, breaking this habit involves breaking down the individual triggers that spark the thoughts that inevitably lead you to the action of drinking alcohol. As we've seen, the alcohol triggers have been built into your life throughout your years of alcohol use. They have become embedded into your subconscious programming and into the sequences of trigger-action-consequence that move you through your day.

Let's take a look at some of the places that might trigger your alcohol use and what you can do about them.

Rerouting Your Situational Triggers

Alcohol reminders are everywhere in your environment. There is no way to avoid them. Pubs and bars, restaurants, supermarkets, liquor stores, billboards and other advertisements, and so on.

One of my biggest triggers was my local bar. Ennis, the town I used to live in the West of Ireland, has lots of pubs in the center, at least 20. I'd be able to pass most of the bars without batting an eyelid because I had never been in them and they didn't hold any attraction for me. But there were a few which were my favorite 'watering holes'. I normally didn't have any problem walking past if I had something to do, but it was always precarious. If I saw someone I knew, or got a look inside and there seemed to be something interesting going on, it would often be enough to put an end to any plans that I might have for the rest of the day.

There are many, many triggers in your environment that can be canceled out by simply avoiding them. When you finish work, you don't have to take the route which brings you by the liquor store or past the pub. You can always find an alternative route, even if it brings you out of your way.

Avoiding Triggering Places Forever?

You don't have to avoid these places forever. Once you've allowed a few weeks to pass, your cravings for alcohol will be much easier to handle. Then, if you still want to travel your old route, if it's more convenient, why not?

Bars and pubs are a different story. If you're going to go back to your local bar, I wouldn't recommend doing it unless you have a reason apart from just sitting at the bar while you're watching other people drinking. Being in a pub, just for the sake of being there, is one of the quickest ways to undo *all* the good work that you've done so far. It's like a heroin user going back to the place where he used to use.

I still go to bars, but I only go to watch football or to eat a meal. Once the game is finished or I've finished eating I won't stay. I've better things to do with my time. It won't take you much time to get into the same mentality!

Your Triggering Times and How To Master Them

"Time changes everything except something within us which is always surprised by change."
Thomas Hardy

Cultural Timing

Time is one of the biggest triggers for any heavy drinker. In our modern world, we live our lives according to the clock. Roughly speaking, we get up in the morning at the same time, we arrive at work at the same time, and finish at the same time in the evening. There are very few drinkers, even heavy drinkers, who don't take time into account.

Culturally, we tend to drink at specific times; in the evening, at the weekend, on our vacations, and so on. Our use of alcohol can be restrained as well as facilitated by the clock. We all have responsibilities and there are times when we just can't drink. We have to go to work, drive the kids to school, and make sure a hundred other tasks are dealt with as part of our regular day.

If you drink every day, you probably have a set time before you'll allow yourself to start drinking. For instance, there's a sort of unwritten rule that if you don't want to be viewed as an alcoholic, you don't start drinking before midday. This gives us the feeling that we are the ones who are in control, and if we're in control then there's no problem.

Being the Ringmaster

My alcohol use fit pretty much into the above profile. I did the majority of my drinking in the evenings, on the weekends, and it was open season as soon we left home for a holiday/vacation. I'd try not to drink before noon, although it didn't take too much convincing for me to break that particular rule. Even though drinking in the morning went against my rulebook, I could easily find an excuse for grabbing a few morning pints once the opportunity had presented itself.

My big magic trick was going alcohol free for the odd day or two. To me, this proved that I was still the ringmaster! Not drinking every day, no matter how much I wanted to, proved to me that I still had it all under my control. What a joke!

How to Deal With Time Triggers

There's not much you can do to avoid time triggers. The evening is still going to come at the end of every day; each week is still going to be capped off by the weekend. If you normally start drinking at six o'clock every night, six o'clock is still going to roll around as regular as clockwork.

To deal effectively with your time triggers, you need to alter the other elements, like what you're doing, where you are, who you're with, and what you're thinking or saying to yourself.

Once you tune in to your habit, you'll start to spot the sequences of trigger-action-consequence. You might walk through your front door after work, go straight into the kitchen, open the fridge to grab a beer, and then sit front of the TV or at the dining table.

Each of these actions offers you the chance to alter the sequence. For instance, you can go to the gym after work or for a quiet walk. You don't have to go into the kitchen as soon as you come home. You can have fruit juice or bottles of water in your fridge, grabbing one of those instead. Or you can go play with your kids instead of sitting in front of the TV.

The March of Time

You can conquer your time alcohol triggers pretty quickly because, by their very nature, you have to repeat them every single day. You repeat your evening triggers at the end of every day. You repeat your weekend triggers at the end of every week. It won't take very long before these times are triggering new habits. Time solves most things, with a little help from you.

What time of the day sets off your alcohol use? Do you set yourself time constraints around your use, like not drinking before midday? Look at the sequencing of your time triggers. Which parts of the sequence can you alter?

Understanding Your Emotional Alcohol Hot Buttons and How to Calm Them Down

"Negative emotions like loneliness, envy, and guilt have an important role to play in a happy life; they're big, flashing signs that something needs to change."
Gretchen Rubin

Emotional triggers can be some of the most difficult to figure out. As we've seen in the last section, most heavy drinkers use alcohol at a certain time of the day. It doesn't matter if we're happy, sad, pissed off, disappointed, frustrated, guilty, or just tired. As soon as the time is right, we get out the bottle or head to the pub. Our feelings become a mere sideshow.

Of course, we know that our emotions can also trigger our drinking. We tend to drink more frequently or heavily at certain emotional times in our lives. We might drink more heavily when we're feeling depressed or lonely, for instance. Having a great night out and feeling really happy can also mean staying out longer and drinking more alcohol.

Your Emotional Tool Chest

For the most part, we've been using alcohol as a tool to deal with our emotions for years. In some cases, handling difficult feelings in this way becomes the default action.

It's an easy trap to fall into.

When you're faced with difficulties in your life, you have a choice. You can deal with the underlying causes or you can go for the temporary instant gratification solution. The difficulty is that the underlying problem that's causing you to feel stressed might take a lot of effort and time to resolve. What do you do in the meantime? Alcohol gives you the opportunity to release the tension for a while, to forget, and to offset your pain for another day. You might tell yourself, "I'll have the instant gratification now and I'll deal with the problem tomorrow".

Tomorrow never comes.

My Shyness

I discovered very early that I could use alcohol as a way of short circuiting my shyness. I remember the feeling of walking into any public place, particularly crowded bars, and being terrified. I was terrified about how I looked, or what other people were thinking about me, especially the girls. I was self-conscious about how I was walking and talking. I had all the typical teenage worries and doubts about myself.

With a couple of alcoholic drinks inside me, I felt like I could finally open up. Alcohol didn't make me any better at walking or talking, it made me not care about what other people thought about me. With a drink in me, I had bravado. I thought I was cool and that being cool was all that mattered.

I still felt uncomfortable whenever I walked into a bar, but I knew that once I got those first couple of pints tucked away, I'd be alright. I never lost that desire to swallow the first couple of drinks very quickly. Even now that I don't drink alcohol anymore, I still down my first pint of orange juice like I'm dying of thirst.

But alcohol was never the answer to my shyness problem. The shyness never disappeared. Drinking was like putting on a mask. I'd wake up the next morning with all the same fears still intact.

It might sound strange, but it feels like I'm starting to really deal with my shyness for first time. Of course, I'm not that spotty teenager any more, I'm a 48 year old adult. And I understand much more about myself and others. I also have a lot more life experience, so it's not such a drama as it was back then, but I do get my moments. I'm quickly learning how to deal with all sorts of social situations without hiding behind that veil of drunkenness.

I often wonder where I would be now, what type of person I would be emotionally, if I didn't hide from the normal emotional problems that every teenager has to go through.

Where Are Your Emotional Cues?

It's going to be tough for you to isolate your emotional triggers in the beginning because drinking alcohol has become integrated with the normal events like coming home from work, relaxing in front of the TV, or drinking with your meal.

As you go through the days and weeks ahead without a drink, the glue that holds the habit sequences together starts to weaken. Each trigger separates out from the behavior, and the more common alcohol triggers in your life start to lose their associations. Triggers are like a muscle. If you don't use them you lose them.

David's Dinnertime Discomfort

Let's take an example. David always used to drink a glass of beer with his evening meal. Once he stopped using alcohol, he replaced the glass of beer with a glass of water. Now, as he sat down to his evening meal, his 'drink with dinner' trigger was still firing off.

His alcohol-drinking habit expected to receive some very specific feedback each time he lifted the glass to his mouth. His drinking habit eyes expected to see a rich, golden liquid, capped off with a thick and creamy head. Drinker Dave's drinking habit also expected the familiar smell of hops and malt in his nose, the bubbles exploding into a froth on his tongue and down his throat, along with a very distinct and familiar taste.

Instead, what he experiences is a very bland, colorless, and relatively tasteless liquid. Every time he sips from the glass, his habit expects beer but tastes water, and his mind gets irritated. He feels stressed out and uncomfortable when he normally would feel relaxed.

If we look at the atmosphere of a normal evening meal before he quit, he'll go from talking with his family to thinking about the day's events - what happened today in the office, the stupid ignoramus who cut him off on his way home from work, or how much he's looking forward to the family vacation which is only a few weeks away. Now, his attention is being constantly dragged back to this bloody glass of water sitting in front of him, pretending to be his old glass of beer. It's irritating, distracting, and totally disagreeable.

After many repetitions of this, David's mind will get used to the water. His meal times won't trigger thoughts about alcohol any more. And he'll soon return to his previous state of relaxation as the taste of water becomes a part of his norm.

The connection between his beer with dinner and his relaxation at dinner has always been false. All along, his relaxation was brought about because he was finished work, he was in the safe environment of his home, he was in the company of the people who he trusted and felt most relaxed with, and he was about to fill his belly with some good food. The beer played only a minor role in a much greater habit.

David's emotional discomfort without his beer at dinner is just one of the triggers that is part of his daily life. As we've already seen, these triggers are handled very well with just the passage of time. The more time passes, the quicker the trigger loses its sting.

Your Emotional Skillset

Without alcohol acting as your emotional safety blanket, you'll have to deal directly with your emotions as they come up. You can't hide from them any more behind a curtain of fog. This was one of the aspects of quitting drinking that I had the most apprehension about.

In reality, dealing with any emotion is simply a skill or set of skills. If you don't have that particular skill, it's something you can learn. And it's no more difficult to learn the skills you need to handle your emotions than it was to learn any of the other skills you've already acquired.

Think about all the things you can do. You can walk, run, speak a language or two, drive a car, and so on... Learning is just a step-by-step process, but it's a process that we are remarkably adapted to. Throughout our lives, we are capable of learning new skills.

The *'can't teach old dogs new tricks'* saying might apply to old dogs, it certainly doesn't apply to old humans. Older adults can learn just about anything that young adults can learn. We just might use a different part of our brain to do it. Any weaknesses that develop in one part of your brain, as you age, is more than compensated for by moving the learning of that task to another part of your brain. It might take the *old dog* a bit longer, but the capacity to learn is there.

Unwanted Alcohol Thoughts

Some emotions are more difficult to handle than others. When you've been using alcohol to deal with your emotional upsets over the years, it's no surprise that when you get emotionally charged, drinking alcohol can be one of the first thoughts that might pop into your mind. This can happen even many months after you've stopped. This is because your brain still considers getting pissed to be a viable option for dealing with the discomfort of emotional upset.

Please remember that these are just thoughts. Every day, we all have many thoughts that we would never transfer into action. How many times have you thought that you wanted to clobber someone who you perceived had said or done something wrong to you? You may have imagined yourself punching them on the nose or something worse, but you didn't follow through.

When you don't drink anymore, the thoughts that you have about alcohol are just added to that list. Don't be upset by them. Never think that these thoughts are a sign of your impending failure. They're not. Thinking about alcohol, especially in times of stress, is perfectly normal. Just stop what you're doing, take a moment to gather yourself, and allow the alcohol thoughts to gently slide away.

Costly Christmas Sleep-In

One example from my own life happened almost a year after I'd stopped. I'd organized a plane ticket for my son to visit for Christmas. The day of his departure came. I rang him to make sure he was on the bus from Galway to Dublin. The phone just rang out. I thought he might not have heard the phone above the sound of the bus engine, so I called again. And again. And again. No answer. Now I started to panic.

Eventually, about an hour later, I did get an answer. He told me he'd slept in and missed his flight. After a fairly sharp conversation I hung up and started to weigh up my options. Naturally, my first thought was, 'Little Bollocks'! That thought passed quickly and I knew I couldn't leave him on his own in Ireland for Christmas, despite how much I thought it would be a long-lasting lesson. If it were at any other time of the year I would have been tempted.

I was short of money so I couldn't book another flight. I knew I wouldn't get a refund on the ticket because he'd missed the flight. So I called my sister and told her what happened.

The first thing she said was "Don't go back on the booze!"

I must admit, for a split second after I found out he'd missed his flight, I did think about getting pissed. But it was only a passing thought. My lovely sister lent me the money for the new flight. Being that close to Christmas we couldn't book anything direct from Dublin to Alicante. The only option was an overnight stop. Any time he's due to fly over, I remind him of the horrendous night he spent trying to sleep on a cold metal bench in Madrid airport.

It's Only a Suggestion, Not a Demand!

The point is, when you've spent a lifetime dealing with adversity by drinking alcohol, your mind is still going to view alcohol as a plausible alternative when things start to get tough. But that's all that's happening. Getting pissed is an alternative that your mind is throwing in for your consideration. That's how your brain works. It doesn't mean anything sinister about your state of mind, nor does it say you're an alcoholic. This is just normal behavior.

Think about how your drinking is triggered by your emotions. Do you drink when you get pissed off? Are you more likely to use when you're tired at the end of the day, rather than when you have a lot of energy? Do your fears or anxieties push you towards the bottle?

Some of your biggest triggers are the people in your life. In the next section, we're going to look at avoiding certain types of people.

Alcohol Freedom Mindset Four

Communication is Essential for Cooperation Even When It's Uncomfortable or Uneasy

"Knowledge is power. Information is liberating. Education is the premise of progress, in every society, in every family."
Kofi Annan

Communicating With the Closest People In Your Life

As we've seen, as alcohol users, alcohol use becomes an embedded part of our everyday lives. It's part of our culture, our communities, and it can also play a part in our family lives.

Again, finding alcohol freedom is a life-altering decision, which not only affects you, it also affects those who are closest to you. Think about how many different aspects of your life are going to change as a result of not using alcohol. Because your spouse and family share so much of your life, this decision is going to have a heavy impact on them also. The difference is that you've probably been mulling over the problem for a long time, running through different scenarios, and looking at things from alternative angles. You've already taken the time to work out how your life is going to look once you've quit. Your family didn't have this option. When people don't have the right information, they tend to jump to bad conclusions.

Not Spilling Soon Enough

One of the mistakes I made in the beginning of my journey was not telling my family about my decision until the last minute. Of course, Esther and Sean (my son) both knew I drank a lot. They were with me on too many occasions when I got absolutely blathered not to have known that I was a seriously heavy user.

But I didn't tell Esther about my plans until the day before I stopped. Even though I told my son that I thought I was an alcoholic about a week before I quit, I didn't tell him that I had quit until a couple of days after I'd stopped. It took me weeks or even months to tell some of the other members of my family. The timing set Esther on the defensive until she got used to things. And it made the first few weeks more difficult than they otherwise might have been.

Mulling Over the Repercussions

In Mindset One, I said that one major part of successfully stopping drinking alcohol is to first get yourself into the right frame of mind. Spending the time to your head in the right place gives you the chance to think about how things are going to be from now on, in the short term and the long term. You also need to give this same opportunity to the closest people in your life.

A common email I receive is from people who've told their partners about their decision to quit, only to get a negative reaction. They expected to get support from their spouse and what they got was opposition. What's generally happened is that the person who's quitting has left it until the last moment to tell their spouse.

Imagine it from their perspective. They are happily getting along with their lives when out of the blue you tell them that you won't be drinking alcohol any more. What are they going to think? Some of their thoughts might be:

"How do I tell our friends that you've given up alcohol?"
"What will they think?"
"Will they think that we're all alcoholics?"
"How can I enjoy myself if I am the only one drinking?"
"Will you be an insufferable bore now that you don't drink?"
"Are you going to become a different person?"
"What will happen to our marriage?"
"Will you start looking down on me because I still drink?"

Seeing Things from Your Perspective

Opening up in advance gives your family members the opportunity to run through the various rehearsals in their own heads. They can think and talk about any questions they may have, and take the time to come to their own conclusions. The more time you give them to think, the more they are likely to see the logic behind what you're doing and to be on your side when the time comes. You're giving them the chance to get *their* head in the right place.

Take the time to sit down and talk about your decision as soon as you can. Talk about why you're choosing to stop using alcohol, the thought processes that went into the decision, and so on. You can also use this as an opportunity to reassure them that this is your decision, it's your choice, and you're not going to start preaching about how they should also stop drinking. Explain that you're doing this to improve your life as well as theirs.

Who Else Deserves to Be Told about Your New Adventure?

"Lying is an elementary means of self-defense."
Susan Sontag

Who else should you tell? Again, the changes you make now are going to alter your life forever. So when you're deciding who you should or shouldn't tell, take the life-changing nature of what you're doing into account. Reflect on any other life-changing decision that you've made or are likely to make in your life. Who would you tell about these decisions? If you were having a new baby or changing your job or moving house, who would you tell? How much would you tell them?

Tell the people you want to tell and don't bother with the rest. It's none of their business. If you need to tell folks outside your family, simply explain what you're doing and why you're doing it. Let them know that you value them and would like their support. If you don't get that support, so be it!

Don't ever feel the need to explain yourself if you don't want to. When I first quit, I told people that I wasn't drinking because I had to drive or that I was on medication. As a strategy, it worked great. It got me through the first couple of months without having to go into any further explanations or get myself worked up because someone wouldn't stop asking me to have *'just the one'*.

The point is, tell a lie if you need to! Your health is way more important than being honest with people who are of no consequence in the long run. As I said in the last section, anyone who matters will already know about your decision to stop because you've told them. Everyone else is not your concern. Don't upset yourself about it, but rather use your own judgment. If it feels right for you to open up to someone, do it. If it doesn't, don't feel any guilt about it.

The Company You Keep Impacts and Influences Your Choices

"We gain the strength of the temptation we resist."
Ralph Waldo Emerson

Going To the Pub

One of the biggest concerns I hear, and rightly so, is about your social life and what will happen to it. I have to be brutally honest here. If your social life revolved around the bar, and your best mates are drinkers, then something has got to give if you are going to be successful.

Not drinking alcohol and still going to the pub, as if you were still drinking, is not going to work. I'm not saying you can't go to the pub in the future or spend time with your old drinking buddies. It's just not going to be the same. You have to establish some rules for yourself before you start out.

My Pub Visits

I still went to the pub, even in the early days, and I spent time with the lads I used to drink with. But I only went to watch a match. I still continue to do this. I order a pint of orange juice, enjoy the match, and then leave.

During a previous quit attempt, I tried going to the pub after work. Instead of ordering a pint, I ordered a bottle of water or a cup of tea. It was a nightmare. I lasted a couple of weeks. It was so dull and boring. When I was drinking, I could sit in the one spot at a bar for hours. The most I could manage, without the dulling effect of alcohol, was two or three hours. Then I'd have to leave, with relief.

And Drinking Buddies?

What about your drinking buddies? If there are other things you share with these people, outside the pub or drinking, then there's a chance to keep the relationship alive. However, if the friendship is solely based around drinking, it's difficult to see how it can continue.

This is another difficult decision for you to make, but it's essential that you make it, and that you make it quickly. People can be big alcohol triggers and your alcohol-drinking buddies are going to be the biggest. Once you associate someone solely with alcohol, it's hard to break that association. There are several people in my life, who as soon as I see them or hear them, make me think about alcohol. You don't need that type of reminder.

You're starting out on a new chapter of your life. Some people need to be left behind in the last chapter, you can't get around that. At the end of the day, you never know, you might be a good influence. Some of your drinking buddies might have been thinking along the same lines but just haven't had the courage to do something about it. Your actions might spark them to take action.

Leading by Example

This has happened quite a few times since I've stopped. Other people get inspired once they see you haven't backtracked, that you've stuck to your guns. When they see how healthy you're starting to look, and how your life has improved, they begin to envision the possibilities for themselves. It's always very satisfying to me when I've inspired someone to at least cut down on the amount of alcohol that they're drinking or to cut it out altogether.

Alcohol Freedom Mindset Five

Well-Timed Rewards are the Fuel for Lasting Behavior Change

"When we take time to notice the things that go right - it means we're getting a lot of little rewards throughout the day."
Martin Seligman

Old Behaviors and Old Rewards

We've already taken a look at what triggers your drinking behavior. Now we'll focus on actions and rewards.

There's a misconception that alcohol is the reward. Every alcohol-drinking habit follows the same simple sequences: trigger, action, and reward. The sequence begins with one of your personal triggers firing off. This trigger sparks a thought which, in turn, causes you to take action, to go into your *get a drink of alcohol* routine. The action part of your *get a drink of alcohol* routine might be to go to the pub or to the supermarket or to your fridge to get some alcohol. This routine always culminates in you drinking the beer or the wine, etc. But there's a further step. This is where your reward lies.

You don't drink just for the sake of drinking. You drink because you want to achieve something else. When you drink water, you don't drink water for the sake of drinking the water, you drink the water so you can quench your thirst. So the reward of pouring a glass of water is not in the drinking, although this might feel good, the reward is having your thirst quenched.

It's the same with alcohol. You don't drink the alcohol for the sake of drinking the alcohol. You're motivated by something deeper.

Early Rewards

When you first started drinking alcohol, you didn't take those first tentative sips because you liked the flavor. As we all know, most alcoholic beverages come with an acquired taste. You only get this acquired taste after substantial exposure to alcohol. You have to train yourself to overcome your natural responses, ignoring the foul taste and the urge to throw up.

Because you've never drank alcohol before, there is no intrinsic attraction from the alcohol itself. Your interest is more aroused through your beliefs and your expectations. It's most likely that you were triggered into using alcohol through the manipulation or coercion from your peers, a strong desire to defy the authority of your elders, or maybe a sense of experimentation.

The early rewards that you got through using alcohol were both physical and psychological. That first drink might have given you a pleasurable and unfamiliar tingling. You may have felt light-headed and a bit dizzy.

The psychological rewards may have included feeling more grown up, easing the peer pressure you were experiencing in that moment, experimentation, or relieving boredom.

The more you drink, the more habitual it becomes. Over time, your reasons to drink also change. As you get older, your motivation for using alcohol might be to relax in the evening, to deal with stress, to forget, and so on. Alcohol use becomes a part of your identity. You become a 'drinker'.

What Now?

The reward, therefore, is not drinking the alcohol. It's what you *get* from drinking the alcohol. This is great news when you're trying to quit. It shows you that you are in control. It shows you that you don't have a disease, nor do you have a problem that's going to hound you for the rest of your life.

More importantly, once you see that alcohol is only the means by which you are getting to your reward, you can start to think about looking at alternative ways of getting to the same reward.

Everything that you get from drinking alcohol can be found through an alternative. There are much better ways of relaxing, socializing, having fun, sleeping, or forgetting about your troubles for a while. There are far better ways that don't require you to pay a destructive price.

Hidden Rewards

Sometimes, the reward you think you're getting from using alcohol is not what you thought it was.

In an earlier section, I spoke about one of my recurring triggers: finishing work in the evening. I'd start to crave a beer from early afternoon, and the anticipation would grow as the afternoon wore on.

By examining my triggers, the anticipation, and the ultimate reward that I was looking for, I presumed that the primary goal was to drink the pints of beer. In fact, the trigger was dehydration. This trigger was firing off throughout the afternoon because I wasn't drinking enough fluids. Therefore because I was starving myself of water, I was subconsciously building anticipation for a drinking session at the end of my work day. So, the final goal was quenching my thirst.

I had established a ritual without even realizing it. By the time I got to the pub, I was gasping from the thirst. It was the dehydration and dry mouth that made that first pint taste really good. In fact, I used to be so thirsty by the time I got to the bar that I'd swallow the first pint in seconds, hardly drawing breath. Because I was drinking Guinness, and Guinness takes a while to settle, I'd always order two pints for myself, knowing that I could be greedy with the first and 'savor' the second. Every time I went through this routine, I was further reinforcing the trigger and bonding it to the alcohol.

Once I'd figured out that the real reward was curing my dehydration or preventing it in the first place, I simply drank more water during the afternoon. This soon became an automatic action. At the end of the shift, I'd pack all the gear away and drink a half liter of water before I drove off. Doing this killed that particular trigger, and I wasn't thirsty after work anymore. There were other triggers that were driving me to the pub, but they had nothing to do with thirst.

Finally, remember that the greatest reward for quitting drinking is not what you get, but who you become!

Here's a few questions you could start out with.

First ask yourself what are you actually craving? What is the reward you really want? Remember that **alcohol is only the means by which you get to your reward**.

Do you crave company? Are you looking for a way of relaxing? Are you just thirsty? Once you know the real craving, you can tailor the reward to better satisfy your real need.

Reward Yourself Often to Reinforce Your New Habits

"Correction does much, but encouragement does more."
Johann Wolfgang von Goethe

Reshaping Your Life

Now let's take a look at the importance of encouraging your progress by rewarding yourself during the first few weeks of your quit.

When you stop using, there'll be large gaps left in your life that the habit used to fill. This is where most of your discomfort lies. And the majority of that discomfort will be psychological.

Getting through those first few weeks can be tough going. Whole sections of your life are transforming as you migrate away from the habit. The resulting shakedown can mean a rollercoaster of competing forces dragging you from one emotion to another.

There are changes happening in your personal life. Large chunks of time that used to be dominated by drinking alcohol and subsequent recovery, are now free. This is a wonderful feeling - once you get used to it. But that sudden freedom can cause its own problems. What do you do with all the time on your hands? How do you do the things you used to do, only without alcohol, such as celebrating or relaxing? Some people even go into a period of mourning. It can be overwhelming and confusing, but we know this period of change doesn't last long, and time is on your side. As the days go by, your brain will gradually dump the parts of your habit sequence that aren't being reinforced.

You can use rewards in the short term to help you get through this transitioning period.

Regular and timely rewards not only motivate you and make you feel good, they also act as positive reinforcements for the new behaviors you want to bolster. Every time you reward your new behavior, it's like giving it a thumbs-up. The more thumbs-up a behavior receives, the stickier it will become, eventually turning into a new habit.

Punishment

Before we move on, just a quick word on punishment.

There are two types of punishment. The first type of punishment is where something you don't like occurs after a particular behavior. The second type of punishment is where something is taken away from you as a result of a particular behavior.

Feeling ill and vomiting after drinking alcohol is an example of the first. By inducing nausea and vomiting, your biological system is reacting violently because you've just swallowed a poison. This should cause any sane person to come to the conclusion that drinking alcohol is just plain stupid, and force them to resolve never to repeat the process (how fortunate are they!). If vomiting happened every time you drank, you'd have to be an extreme die-hard to want to continue.

An example of the second type of punishment is losing your license after being convicted of drunk driving. It's a form of a penalty administered by the courts because you've broken the law. When I was stopped for drinking and driving, the first thing I did after I was charged and released from the police station, was to go to the pub. But when the reality finally hit home that I was going to lose my license, I had no hesitation in stopping drinking for 10 months.

By the time I'd started drinking again, we'd moved to a part of town that was within walking distance of the pubs. The punishment of losing my license only worked on me because it threatened my livelihood. I couldn't work if I couldn't drive. I often wonder if that was part of the reason I started working on an alternative career, which I could practice from home with no danger of a DUI.

These are two examples of penalties which are dealt out by forces which are beyond our control. Can self-administered punishments be just as effective?

Self-Administered Punishments

One of the reasons I don't think self-punishment works too well is because it doesn't help in teaching you the new behaviors that you need to learn. Punishment only suppresses the old behavior.

Another reason is that punishment won't make you feel good. It only makes you feel like you're a failure, someone who doesn't deserve anything, or you're missing out on things, etc.

While you're in that discomfort zone of the first couple of weeks, it's easy to think that you're depriving yourself of a real pleasure. The last thing you need is something that adds to that feeling of deprivation.

Self-Maligning Language

I include negative self-talk in this category of self-administered punishment. What many people would think of as 'straight talk' can often be bordering on being abusive. Life can be tough enough without castigating yourself.

Think about how you would react if someone else were trying to motivate you by using insulting language. What would you do? Would you calmly accept it or would you knock their block off? If you wouldn't accept that kind of talk from someone else, don't accept it from yourself.

Sometimes you need to straight-talk yourself into pushing on, despite the discomfort. But all-stick-and-no-carrot won't motivate you in the long run.

How Should You Reward Yourself?

The best types of reward always make you feel good. They should also be given as close as possible to the behavior you're trying to reinforce or when you reach your target.

First, choose the event that you want to reward. The event might be a benchmark or a goal that you are aiming at. Let's say you want to reward yourself for getting through the first few days. Start by buying a daily calendar. You can download a calendar free from the Alcohol Mastery website here. If your goal is to get through the first day, mark off the hours as they pass. Also, make a note on the calendar of the reward you're going to give yourself once you reach your target. For instance, once you get past your first day, you might watch a good movie. Pass the second day, you eat a special meal. Past the third day, you buy yourself something nice.

You could also reward yourself after you've overcome a particularly heavy feeling of craving.

If you would normally open your first drink at 4 o'clock in the afternoon, once that specific time has passed, reward yourself by doing something enjoyable.

How are you going to reward yourself?

What Should Your Rewards Be?

Your rewards can be anything you want, but they must have some personal meaning to you. There's no point in rewarding yourself with something you don't want. Your reward could be something that you buy for yourself, a concert ticket, a limo ride, a trip to the movies, a DVD or book. Another form of reward is something that money can't buy, suck as extra time playing with the kids, flying a kite, or just spending a couple of hours sitting alone in an easy chair reading a novel or listening to some music.

What will you reward yourself with?

Try to follow the event closely with the reward. If you're rewarding yourself for overcoming a strong urge to drink, don't wait for an hour after the urge has successfully passed before you give yourself the reward. The reinforcement will be much stronger if you reward yourself immediately.

Sometimes it's just not practical to reward yourself right away. You might be at work or driving your car. If you can't take it immediately, then find some other way of at least acknowledging the reward in that moment. Maybe you could make a mark in a notebook every time you overcome a craving. When you have ten marks, you're entitled to one reward, to be taken at your convenience.

Jo's Fridge Sock

Jo is one of our Australian Alcohol Masters. At the time of writing this book, she has almost completed the first year of her new journey. Part of her reward scheme was saving the money she would have otherwise spent on booze. She hung a big colorful sock on the outside of her fridge door and set a timer to go off every hour. As soon as she heard the timer, she'd put a dollar into the sock.

Not only was she saving up for something special in the future, she had a jingling reminder of how good her new life was every time she opened the fridge door.

Cautions

A couple of caveats are worth noting here. You must be totally honest with yourself. You're building new habits, after all. If you try to cheat, you're undermining all your long-term goals. So don't take the reward if you haven't completed the desired behavior.

And try to refrain from rewarding yourself with food or drinks. This is a behavior that can all too readily turn into another bad habit like comfort eating, which could lead to more problems in the future.

Alcohol Freedom Mindset Six

Everything You Want is on the Other Side of Your Fears

"It is not the most intellectual of the species that survives; it is not the strongest that survives; but the species that survives is the one that is able to adapt to and to adjust best to the changing environment in which it finds itself"
Leon C. Megginson

Many people who know they have a problem with alcohol will never get to the action stage because they associate too much fear and pain with stepping across the starting line.

Fear and Pain

One type of pain happens because the instant gratification that alcohol used to provide is now gone, but the habit structures that supported the behavior are still in place.

Fear of the Unknown

Another type of pain comes from the fear of the unknown. This type of fear readily feeds from the brain-washing and miscommunication that we feel when we associate stopping using alcohol with the so-called 'symptoms', 'cravings', 'side effects', 'recovery' and 'relapse'. It also includes the fear of never being able to drink alcohol again, or specifically the fear of just 'being sober'.

This was one of my biggest fears before I stopped. The idea of never being able to have a drink again certainly scared me. This fear probably played a large part in why I always searched out and believed any piece of 'research', sensationalist 'journalism', that offered the slightest hint that there might be a healthy benefit to alcohol consumption. As soon as I read something I liked the sound of, I didn't need any further proof. It just became a solid part of my alcoholic version of reality.

Behind it all was a deep fear of being without my safety blanket.

Fear of Incompetence

A third type of fear comes about because people set themselves up with such lousy expectations of their own future. They believe that there's a massive gulf between where they are now and where they want to be. They also believe that they don't have the personal abilities to bridge that behavioral gulf.

Fear of the Future

On a similar line, and maybe worse, is the fear that all the good times are now in the past. People who have this fear believe that there's no escaping the damage that's already been done, that they'll stay addicted to and be a victim of this ridiculous drug for the rest of their lives. They believe that they will never have a successful life outcome! Even if they fight the urges forever, never having another drop of booze again, they will always feel like they are missing out on something that they desperately want.

What kind of life is that?

Closer to the Truth!

The truth is that you were fine before you ever started using alcohol and you'll be fine once you stop using alcohol. It just takes time!

Here are real Truths:

If you permanently stop breathing, you're in big trouble.
If you permanently stop eating, you're in big trouble.
If you permanently stop drinking, you're in big trouble.
If you permanently stop drinking alcohol, you're free!

Breathing, eating, and drinking are needs that are essential to your life. Drinking alcohol only feels like a need!

Breathing, eating, and drinking are normal things to do. There's nothing normal about drinking alcohol!

The truth is that from the moment you stop drinking alcohol, you're free.

It might take some time for your body and mind to adjust, but it will adjust. That's just the way you are designed. Your system is constantly trying to find a balance. There's always going to be a period of adjustment that brings with it a certain amount of discomfort. Think about this as stepping into your discomfort zone. That discomfort zone is the feeling of your body transforming you from the person you are into the person you want to be.

Taking the Easy Road

As heavy drinkers, we've been taking the easy way out for years. The immediate satisfaction of our needs has taken precedence over sound judgment. As with most things in life that provide instant gratification, after the buzz has gone, there's always a payment to be made, like a sting of venom left behind waiting to be released.

ALCOHOL FREEDOM • 94

The more you gratify your needs in the present, the more venom is building up for the future.

Think of it like a credit card. You buy what you want right now, regardless of whether you've earned the money to pay for it or not. Each purchase adds to the overall debt. The more you buy, the more debt you accumulate. Soon the high rate of interest is added to the equation and the debt accumulates all on its own.

Such is an alcohol habit. The alcohol debt gathers momentum the more you drink. Eventually, the damage caused by the alcohol enters the equation, you need to drink alcohol just to feel normal. Finally, the debt catches up with you, and you have to pay the piper!

This type of instant gratification mentality has to stop. You must start to pay first and play later.

Expect What's Right

You need to set yourself up with positive expectations from the start. Henry Ford said *"If you think you can do a thing, or think you can't do a thing, you're right!"* The expectations you set for yourself, before you begin with any action, will play a large part in the outcome of that action. Make the choice to perceive the discomfort, the transformation, and the adjustments as clear signs that your body is healing and that your mind is forcing the habit to collapse.

Negative Language

As I said earlier in this book, you should get some proper medical advice, even if you do so for no other reason than to put your mind at rest. But once you leave the doctor's office, make sure you leave words like 'withdrawal' and 'side-effects' to the doctor and to the medical-forms. Your doctor needs to use terms like that for the insurance payments and for their own records. You shouldn't use

ALCOHOL FREEDOM • 95

these words to describe your own situation because they set you up with negative expectations. Let's take an example.

What images does the word 'withdrawal' conjure up in your mind? Hospitals, doctors, pain, medication, suffering, a drug addict sweating and shaking uncontrollably while he goes through the nightmare of cold turkey.

Now think about a person in transition. How do you picture that person?

If you think about the processes of stopping drinking alcohol, not as a withdrawal but as a transition, you'll generate a perception in your mind of something that's more confident and more achievable.

A transition sounds promising, adventurous, appealing, and full of possibilities. It sounds like something you want to dive into straight away.

Withdrawal conjures up images of terrible pain and misery. It sounds like something that is completely out of your control.

A transition sounds like something you can handle. It sounds like something that you can control.

Float Like a Butterfly

The first thought that comes to my mind when I think about transition is the metamorphosis of a caterpillar changing into a butterfly. When I stopped drinking, it felt like that - like a personal metamorphosis. I started out feeling like I was cocooned inside a world that was choking the life out of me. I was surrounded by a growing mountain of difficulties and problems that always seemed insurmountable. Once I understood that all those problems originated from my drinking alcohol, it was easy to push myself to stop, to push myself out of the cocoon and breathe the fresh air.

Try this experiment: Go to Google and type the word *withdrawal* into the search box. When the results come back, go to the top of the page and click on the images tab. What do you see? For me, the first picture is a black and white image of a woman sitting in a corner looking desperate. The second image is of a woman silently screaming and pulling at her hair. The third is a picture of another frail looking man lying on the ground reaching for an open bottle of pills. These are the types of images that we would typically associate with the word withdrawal. It's all about pain, desperation, depression, darkness, and so on. If you think about your process in terms of 'withdrawal', this is what you're going to see in your imagination. How can you not fear this kind of harrowing future? Even though you have really only conjured this up in your own mind, it will still produce very strong emotional reactions. Go watch any horror movie and you'll see people who are feeling all the signs of fear, despite the fact that they know what they're watching is not real. The human mind is a powerful tool.

Now go through the same Google search, as you did before, this time searching for the word *transition*. Type 'transition' or 'transformation' or 'adaptation' into the Google box and take a look at the image results. Do you see the difference? There are smiling faces, images of strength, growth, evolution, brightness. It's all about change, movement, new life, possibilities, metamorphosis, and so on.

Listening to 'Authority'

The point is, you get to choose how you perceive things and how you interpret those perceptions. It's your brain after all. The language you use to define your experience plays a massive role in how you come to your initial perceptions. And your initial perceptions color the meaning of everything that follows.

For instance, one authoritative paper, written by four M.D.'s, called *Complications of Alcohol Withdrawal**, states that "serious withdrawal symptoms occur in approximately 10 percent of patients. These symptoms include a low-grade fever, rapid breathing, tremor, and profuse sweating."

Anatomy of a Hangover

I wonder if these doctors ever had a hangover. Every morning after I'd drunk too much, I woke up with a low-grade fever, rapid breathing, tremor, and profuse sweating. As well as that, I'd almost always wake feeling like I wanted to vomit. I felt depressed, lethargic, and on and on. All this time I was getting *serious withdrawal symptoms*. And I thought it was a just hangover!

When I quit alcohol for good, I didn't have any serious withdrawal symptoms, except I couldn't sleep. Maybe that was partly due to not having a skin full of alcohol the night before I stopped, so I didn't have a hangover.

Did you ever stop to think about what a hangover actually is? It's such an integrated part of drinking, and drinking culture, that we take it for granted.

For me, there are two ways to look at a hangover.

Type A. Your body is withdrawing from the alcohol. Your need for alcohol is making you shake, sweat, and breath irregularly. Cure: Drink more alcohol immediately (the hair of the dog). Once you have more alcohol in your system, the dreaded withdrawal will disappear. All you have to do is rinse and repeat!

Type B. Your body is shocked by the amount of alcohol you've just consumed. You've been poisoned and your body has spent the last few hours trying to deal with that poisoning. Consequently, you feel the trauma, shaking, sweating, and irregular breathing. Cure: Don't drink any more alcohol and you'll never have another hangover.

Throughout my drinking life, I thought about my hangover as Type A. I would always follow the serious hangover with the hair of the dog. And I was convinced it worked. Then I stopped drinking. To my amazement, I found that once I didn't swallow any more alcohol, I never had another hangover again.

Death by Withdrawal: A Comparison

I'm sometimes accused of not giving enough attention to the risks of death by withdrawal syndrome. I understand that there is a risk, but what is that risk exactly? It's hard to find conclusive facts.

Huge numbers of people are dying prematurely from alcohol *use* every year. The enormity of this problem is further pronounced by the many deaths from alcohol that are not reported as such. For instance, the reason a person has died may have been their years of alcohol use. But the actual event that triggered the death was heart failure. Subsequently, when the death certificate comes to be drawn up, the cause of death will be listed as heart failure, not alcohol related. Although they have technically died from heart failure, the real cause was drinking alcohol over many years. In other words, the alcohol use over many years has done significant damage to the body, including the heart, and it's this damage that caused the heart to fail.

In the same way, with death from alcohol withdrawal, technically the person has died from the sudden shock of alcohol cessation. They drank alcohol and they were alive, then they stopped drinking alcohol and they died. The cause and effect is conveniently made simple. In reality, they have died because of the thousands of gallons of this poison that they've poured into their bodies over many years.

Those who are at risk of dying from suddenly stopping drinking alcohol are in a small minority. However, this isn't the picture that is painted by the quit alcohol industry or by many top-level health websites.

My question has always been: Why do medical websites put so much emphasis on the risks of quitting alcohol?

Let's look at a comparison, a condition that causes a similar percentage of deaths.

Almost 4% (772,000) of all patients who were admitted to hospital in the United States, in 2011, contracted a healthcare associated infection or hospital acquired infection (HAI)**. Out of those 772,000 patients who contracted an HAI, approximately 75,000 (10%) of the patients succumbed to the infection and died. So in a single year, 75,000 patients died in hospital as a result of an infection that they got while they were in the hospital.

The percentage of people who are at risk from alcohol withdrawal is approximately 4%, roughly the same percentage as those who contracted an HAI. Of the 4% who are vulnerable to very serious alcohol withdrawal, about 5% will die. This is half the percentage of those who end up dying from an HAI.

When you go online to search for healthcare information about an upcoming hospital visit like a surgical procedure to remove an ingrown toenail, you won't be told about the risks of your hospital stay, that you have a 4% chance of catching an HAI, or that you run the risk of paying the ultimate price of death by HAI.

Why not?

Because it would undermine the whole medical system. Why is it acceptable for almost every healthcare site that provides information about quitting drinking to place details about the risks of death from alcohol withdrawal in such a prominent position?

Is it the way these risks are interpreted? Is it just perception? Is it the money?

Is it because you can't perform toenail surgery on yourself? (Most of us can't at any rate.) There's no competition for that type of service. You have to go to a doctor.

But you *can* quit drinking on your own, as most people, in fact, do. **At least 75% of alcohol users who stop using do so without any outside help.**

Question: How do you convince someone that they need the services of an expensive healthcare clinic or dry-out center and that a person should never try to quit on their own? Answer: By telling them the 'risks' of death if they try to quit drinking alcohol on their own.

Again, if you have any doubts, then obtain independent medical advice. I think most people can quit on their own. The rates of success for those who haven't sought out medical help are well documented. The same cannot be said for those who have failed. But I have to stress that I'm not telling you not to go to your doctor. Alcohol-drinking does the damage. If you are at risk from suddenly stopping, it's because of the culmination of all the alcohol you have drunk thus far. I'll go back to the one basic fact that I know to be true: ALCOHOL CAUSES DAMAGE! The only way you can be sure about the amount of damage that has been caused is to have yourself medically checked out. Don't play games with your health.

Half Full or Half Empty: Where Are You?

Let's take a look at the difference between positive and negative thinking and the difference it can make to your efforts.

With glass-half-full thinking (positive thinking), you might view stopping drinking alcohol as the beginning of a series of alterations that are going to change and improve your life. If you have this type of positive thinking, your life will change from a life where all the fun relies on some fake genie in a bottle into a life worth living, the start of something brilliant. Half-full thinkers see the discomfort as a process of transition. This feeling of discomfort is your old habit dying and the new habit taking over and becoming dominant.

Glass-half-empty thinkers, on the other hand, constantly look backwards at what they are going to miss about their old lives. If you concentrate your focus on the past, all you will be able to see is the alcohol and partying and good times you've got to sacrifice or give up or quit for the sake of your health or your family or whatever reason. Half-empty thinking means instead of putting up with the discomfort, you can only see withdrawal symptoms. It means endless cycles of recovery. It means being trapped into a lifetime of wanting but never having.

Take Great Care with Your Wording

The words you use, whether out loud or in your head, affect the way you think. The way you think affects the way you act. The way you act affects the quality and quantity of your life. Choose your words carefully!

I chose the words Onwards and Upwards to represent what Alcohol Mastery is all about. Mastering alcohol in your life is not about quitting drinking this shit. To stop putting the stuff into your body is just the first step. The real mastery is understanding that we've had a twisted relationship with a deadly poison called alcohol right up until this moment. *All our lives we've perceived alcohol as being a normal part of our culture, when in fact we've been conned by the propaganda from white collar drug dealers.*

Ironically, you become an Alcohol Master only when you turn your back on alcohol, on your old ways. Onwards and Upwards is the opposite of the alcoholic lifestyle which is backwards and downwards. This alcoholic lifestyle only leads downwards to an early grave.

Finally, remember that any transition takes effort. Put in that effort and you'll spend a relatively small amount of time in your discomfort zone. Then you have alcohol freedom!

In the rest of this section, we'll take a look at a few things you can do to make the transition easier.

* pubs.niaaa.nih.gov/publications/arh22-1/61-66.pdf
** http://www.cdc.gov/HAI/surveillance/

The Biggest Drinking Trigger of Them All

"Water is the driving force of all nature."
Leonardo da Vinci

Alcoholic Diuresis

One of the greatest myths about alcohol is that it quenches your thirst. Alcohol is a diuretic. This means that alcohol dehydrates you at a cellular level and then makes you pee.

Alcohol-induced diuresis should cause a lot of concern for the heavy drinker. The diuretic effect of alcohol involves another round of chemical mess-ups in your system. Your water balancing setup is tricked into believing that there's too much water in your body, hence your frequent trips to the toilet.

Thirsty?

In an earlier chapter, I spoke about how I was always thirsty after I had finished work for the day, and how that thirst pushed me to the pub. I wasn't consciously aware of it at the time. It was only after I had stopped using that I realized that most of those gagging-for-a-pint moments were really only triggers for me to drink some *hydrating* fluid.

Once you stop drinking, you should be aware that many of your so-called cravings for alcohol are nothing more than your natural thirst instincts kicking in. Your body is not telling you to get alcohol, it's simply asking for a nice cool drink of water. You should be drinking at least two liters of water a day (eight eight ounce glasses or half a gallon). If you don't drink enough, you will get dehydrated. The general rule is half an ounce for every ounce of body weight, so a 150 pound person should consume 75 ounces of water.

Hydration Means More than Quenching Your Thirst

Even mild dehydration can make you feel tired with no energy. And when you're tired it's more difficult to think, to act, or to keep on track with your goals. Staying hydrated will help keep you sharp in your mind and body. Our physical and mental performance starts to become impaired once our bodies reach about 1% water loss.

How do you know if you've drunk enough water?

Thirst is one of the last signals of dehydration. A good test is the color of your pee, or lack of color. Your pee should be colorless, or, at the very least, light yellow. If your pee is dark yellow, you're dehydrated, no matter what your mouth is telling you.

Unfamiliar Drinking

At first, when you're trying out new non-alcoholic drinks, it will feel uncomfortable. That's just because you're not used to it. You're accustomed to the taste of beer or wine or whatever. It took me a while before I acclimatized, but it did happen. This is another part of your discomfort zone. Stick with it. Water is not an acquired taste like alcohol. We are born with the taste for water, although we might have to reacquire the taste. More importantly, we're born with the need for water. The average adult is made of about 65% water. When you start feeling thirsty, you've already lost about 3% of your body's overall water supply. Like we saw earlier, your judgment and mental performance is already showing signs of decline at 1% dehydration. To keep yourself strong, keep yourself hydrated.

Soft Drinks?

Getting alcohol out of your life is one of the greatest single improvements you can make. Now that you have done it, you should focus more of your attention to other areas where you can reduce your self-harm footprint. For the sake of your long-term health, and your liver, when you're looking for an alternative drink, don't switch to soft drinks. Fizzy drinks are linked with obesity, fatty liver syndrome, diabetes, heart disease, to name a few. This is especially true if you've been diagnosed with liver issues.

And if you think that your favorite diet soda is any less damaging, think again. Sugar substitutes have been linked with all sorts of nasty conditions. When you are thirsty, the best thing to drink is water. Pure and simple! If you need to add some taste, go for natural fruit juices, or look for the most organic commercial drinks you can find.

Alcohol Trigger Diverting Distraction in Action

"Cure for an obsession: get another one."
Mason Cooley

Alcohol Triggers Again

Let's take another look at your alcohol triggers and a technique called trigger-diverting. The idea behind trigger-diverting is to divert the focus of your triggers away from your normal alcohol-drinking action and onto something less destructive.

As we've seen, an alcohol trigger is any stimulus that creates a thought for alcohol. That thought leads to the action of you drinking alcohol. Finally, you get to your reward. We've also seen that you have two types of triggers, routine triggers and ambush triggers.

For our purposes here, we're going to concentrate on the routine triggers. We want to examine the link between the routine trigger and the action, between the thought of using alcohol and the actual alcohol-drinking. Once you've reached the drinking alcohol action stage, it's too late.

Routine triggers take time to redirect or eliminate because they're an established part in your life. They occur and are reinforced day after day. But they're also the easiest form of trigger to deal with because you will be altering them as you go about your normal life.

Routine Trigger-Breaking

Let's take just one example of a trigger: your finish-work-trigger.

You have decided that you are going to pack in alcohol-drinking once and for all. Too many things have been going wrong in your life, you're getting grief from your wife and boss, and you've been suffering from some pretty terrible hangovers of late. You've gone through your planning stage, your head is in the right place, and you've locked in your alcohol freedom date to the following Monday.

First Week

Alcohol Freedom Monday morning arrives and you're raring to go. You didn't drink too much on your last night and you wake up feeling good about the day ahead. You go to work and as the day progresses you don't feel any discomfort at all.

At the end of your working day - as you pack away your tools, or you close your office door, or you sit in your car for the drive home - the *finished work for the day* alcohol trigger kicks off. This is the first time all day that you've even thought about drinking. Whereas you would normally follow through with your drinking behavior, you're now going to stick an interruption into the habit sequence between the trigger and the action. Instead of the *finished work for the day* alcohol trigger automatically leading you to the *use alcohol* action, the *finished work for the day* alcohol trigger will now lead to a different action, which is the one that you've planned for. That action might be going to the gym, taking the dog for a walk, swimming, surfing, dancing, and so on. This is a where all your preparation and planning is going to pay off. If you haven't completed this preparation and planning yet, go back to Mindset One, which you can find at the start of this book.

Even with the prep work and planning, you're still going to feel uncomfortable. No two people are going to feel the same level of discomfort, but if you've worked your way through the stage of getting your head in the right place, you won't have too much difficulty. There will always be some form of discomfort, but we'll deal with that later in the book. For now, let's get back to your first Monday of alcohol freedom.

Every time you've finished work before today, you haven't needed to think about what action to take. As soon as the *finished work for the day* alcohol trigger fires off, you automatically head in the direction of the pub or the liquor store or the fridge, to get your fix and reward.

Now, you have to think about what you're going to do. Your mind will be seeking your habitual action of going to the pub, the liquor store, your fridge. Your job is to take an alternative action, one that doesn't have to (and may not) be comfortable. Simply put one foot in front of another and perform an act: walking the dog, swimming, or shooting hoops are a few ideas. Use your creativity.

As you make progress through the first week, the strength and influence of that *finished work for the day* trigger decreases by a small amount every day, as does your discomfort. By the time Tuesday evening arrives, when your *finished work for the day* alcohol trigger fires off, it will be slightly easier to deal with because you didn't follow through with the sequence on Monday. On Wednesday, you'll feel slightly less discomfort. On Thursday, slightly less again, and on Friday, less still.

Congratulations!

At this stage, you should just stop for a moment to acknowledge your achievement. Pat yourself on the back. You've just completed a full week of successfully diverting your *finished work for the day* alcohol triggers. As you start afresh the next Monday, you'll have a full week of *not using alcohol* experience behind you. This experience is going to be invaluable going forward. Getting through the past week has given you a reference point about what to expect for the next week. Your discomfort won't be as strong because you partly know what to expect. The foundations for your new habits are well in place and those foundations are getting stronger. So is your resolve.

You've found some of your personal weak spots, the places where your 'cravings' hit the hardest, and you can change things around a bit to avoid those weak spots. You just experienced a full week of alcohol freedom. Now you know you can do it.

First 30 Days

By the end of your first 30 days, you'll have gone through 20 to 25 repetitions of breaking that one sequence between the *finished work for the day* trigger and *use alcohol* action. You've also gone through as many, if not more, repetitions of the many other routine triggers in your life. Examples of these might include the *drink a beer with dinner* trigger, or the *drink a glass of wine before bed* trigger, and so on. You should be able to think of plenty of your own alcohol triggers at this stage.

Now you are gathering strength upon strength and momentum upon momentum as you build a clear picture of what it's like not to use alcohol. This is great feedback and proof that you don't need to use alcohol to get through your life. Your alcohol freedom journey has well and truly begun! You are now over the first hurdles!

Diverting Triggers

So let's take a closer look at this tool to help you drive a wedge between your trigger and action.

Trigger-diverting is any technique that diverts the focus and aim of the trigger away from your normal *use alcohol* action, towards a more suitable action. This alternative action needs to be simple, easy to implement, and instant.

Think about a trigger-diverter as a permanent, internal traffic diversion. The role of the trigger-diverter is to close off access to the old alcohol use route, diverting traffic around the behavior of drinking alcohol, and rejoining the sequence at the reward.

Motivating Emotions

Breaking the sequence, as we've seen, has an impact on your emotions. Your interpretation of these emotions is where you risk being yanked back to your old life. For instance, if you're not sleeping properly over your first few days, there's a chance that you're going to feel tired. That tiredness might cause you to wonder how long this interrupted sleep is going to take. This can stir up your emotions.

One way to interpret your lack of sleep is that your body needs to drink alcohol to sleep. You've always had your little nightcap, and you can't sleep without that nightcap, which means you're probably never going to get a proper night's sleep again.

Alternatively, you can interpret your lack of sleep as your body *adjusting* to the absence of alcohol. Your body is hyperactive in *eliminating* the remaining alcohol. It's making the *necessary reparations* to your internal organs, to your mind, and to your natural rhythms. These changes won't take too long. The last dregs of alcohol will *soon be gone*. Your body *will repair* itself, and then you'll be having the *best sleep* you've had in a long time.

A trigger-diverter is a simple method of controlling your emotions in the first few days and weeks.

Trigger-Diverter Setup

How do we set up a trigger-diverter?

The simplest form of controlling your emotions is dis-traction. The simplest form of distraction is action.

Take a look at these words:

- **Emotion**
- **Motiv**ation
- **Motion**
- Re**move**
- **Act**
- **Act**ion
- Distr**act**ion
- Re**act**ion

Each of these words is derived from the same foundation - the Latin *movere* which means 'to move' and *actionem* meaning 'a putting into motion; a performing, doing'.

Your most fundamental emotions are wired into your brain with the primary purpose of causing a reaction. The triggers for these emotions are buried so deeply into the oldest part of your brain that they fire off way before your logical brain is even aware of what's happening. These automatic reactions are often described as the fight-or-flight response.

Imagine you're sitting still in a quiet room, minding your own business, reading a book or watching some TV. Suddenly there's a loud bang behind you. What's your immediate response? You jump and you look towards the noise. Perhaps you make a dive away from the bang.

Alternatively, imagine you're walking down a dark street on your way home from work. You're alone and you feel slightly on edge. Out of the corner of your eye, you spot a barely perceptible movement in the bushes. Your reaction is immediate. You don't stop to think. You move first and think later.

This motion is at the root of a trigger-diverter. The rule is as follows: You can use motion to control any emotion.

What happens to you when you feel discomfort? How do you feel? What do you think? How do you act and react? If you focus on the discomfort, what happens? Does it go away? No. If you focus your energy on any form of discomfort, you give it power. You concentrate your energy onto a single spot, like a magnifying glass concentrates the energy of the sun onto a piece of paper. If you feel like having a drink and you focus on that feeling or those thoughts, they won't go away. But if you refocus your mind elsewhere, anywhere else, the likelihood is that you'll stop thinking about the drink. If your mind drifts back to the drink, you simply think about something else again.

Sometimes it's difficult to refocus your mind, and bring your thoughts away from something that has a strong attraction. This is where a trigger-diverter comes in.

A trigger-diverter acts as a simple distraction to your drinking thoughts. The best form of distraction is to take an action. You can dance, sing, jump, talk, walk, play, connect with your family or friends or pets, build a bonfire, jump around like a lunatic, tell a story in a stupid voice, jog, swim, or just do something, anything. By using movement, you motivate your emotions into motion. When your emotions are moving, they can't be focused on drinking.

When you move, you alter your state of mind. When you change the scene, you change the act.

My Personal Trigger-Diverter

My ultimate trigger-diverter is walking. It's not the only one I use. I also like to move like an idiot, jumping around, waving my arms and legs like a loony member of Monty Python. It works for me because it makes me laugh! Above all, taking a walk is a sort of cure-all strategy that lifts me up when I need lifting, brings me down when I need grounding, helps me on occasion to think, and, at other times, to quiet my mind.

I can't tell you how much the simple act of just taking a walk has helped to shift my perception away from a triggering moment. Walking is one of the first things we learn to do. It's almost as natural as breathing or eating.

Walking fulfils the criteria for a successful trigger-diverter: it's simple, it's easy to implement, and you can start doing it instantly. You don't need any special equipment or clothing. You can walk wherever and whenever you feel the need. You have all the training you are ever going to require. You can vary your walking to suit your mood and your goals.

As soon as you feel the trigger biting, you can just get up, slip on your shoes (or not) and go for a walk. Nothing can be easier. Don't ponder about what you're thinking or why you're getting the trigger, just get up off your ass and take a walk. If you want to listen to music on your iPod, fine. If you want to make a funny walk, fine. Walk fast, slow, sideways, backwards, over hills, down the street, for a block, a mile, or a marathon... it's up to you.

Your Ability to Respond: The 100% Responsibility Rule

"You cannot escape the responsibility of tomorrow by evading it today."
Abraham Lincoln

A big part of liberating yourself from alcohol is in choosing the direction you want to go from now on and targeting which goals you want to achieve in your future. Without that end destination to aim for, you have no direction. Without a direction, you can spend the rest of your life spinning around in circles, or endlessly drifting from one thing to another.

Where Are You?

We'll talk about the importance of having a plan in the next section. For now, let's dig a little deeper into how you've come to where you are right now.

Every journey has a destination. To get to that destination, you must first know where you're starting from. And to truly understand where you're starting from, where you are right now, you need to know where you've come from, and the path you took to get here.

Every alcohol habit is constructed and reinforced one drink at a time. Nobody takes their first alcoholic drink thinking that one day they're ever going to rely so heavily on this toxin. Nobody starts out thinking that somewhere in the distant future they'll be facing life or death decisions about their drinking.

Part of our cultural acceptance comes from a cultural refusal to think about alcohol as a drug. We think of it as a beverage, like cola, milk, or even water.

Another reason why we're so casual about our use is that using alcohol is culturally linked to common, happy occasions. We all want to be happy so it doesn't take a huge leap for us to equate happiness with drinking alcohol.

Almost all alcohol marketing is devised around this concept. Alcohol companies want to hammer this link - between alcohol and fun times - deep into our group subconscious. The CEO of Distilled Spirits Council of the United States (DISCUS), Peter Cressy, says that "DISCUS is working to ensure cultural acceptance of alcohol beverages by "**normalizing**" them in the minds of consumers as a healthy part of a normal lifestyle." [Emphasis mine]

100% Responsibility Rule

From your point of view, you are where you are because of the cumulative effects of the drug that you've put into your body over the years. When we first start drinking, it's pretty easy to stick to the guidelines of having no more that X number of drinks in any one session and no more than X number of drinks in any one week. It's easy because we haven't built a taste or a tolerance for alcohol yet.

The problem is that alcohol is a drug and it acts just like any other drug. On the one hand, your body fights against the alcohol, treating it as a foreign toxin that must be eliminated. On the other hand, alcohol lowers inhibitions, making the second drink easier to accept than the first, the third easier to accept than the second, etc.

Many of us tell ourselves that we drink alcohol because of how and where we were raised. It's a part of our 'cultural identity'. We drink because our families drink, our peers drink, society deems it as normal to drink, and so on. The reality is that we drink alcohol because it's acceptable to our personal beliefs and self-concepts. Beliefs and self-concepts are very flexible and in the right circumstances can be changed rapidly.

My Alcohol Beliefs

For years, I thought of myself as a drinker. I believed that I would always be a drinker because that's just who I was. Alcohol was a part of my cultural heritage, a part of my family, and a part of my personal identity. How could I remove alcohol from my life and still be me?

It's only now that I have stopped drinking alcohol that I've realized how much those drinking beliefs only served to restrict my life. They were never really true! They were only statements of a reality that I *thought* was true. I'm still 'me' with or without the alcohol. The only difference is that now I'm not handcuffed by the burden of having to plan my life around taking a drug, being high on that drug, or dealing with the consequences of taking that drug.

Your Alcohol Beliefs

In the same way, *your* alcohol beliefs have been a restrictive frame around all of *your* behaviors, *your* emotions, *your* thoughts, and *your* actions for most of *your* life. Those beliefs have placed *you* into an ever-shrinking box that has served only to limit and regulate *your* possibilities.

Eliminate the Beliefs, Eliminate the Want

Eradicate those old beliefs from your mind and everything else will change.

If all you do is get rid of the alcohol, but you still hold onto the beliefs, you won't win at this game because you'll always be aching for a hit that is very easy to get. This is where so-called dry alcoholics fail. They might not have touched a drop of alcohol for 15 years, but they still believe they're addicted to the stuff. They still believe that all it takes is one drink and they'll be right back to where they started.

After two years and the right frame of mind, I can tell you that the thought of actually drinking alcohol *never* crosses my mind. So I know it's all in the head. I *never* think that one drink is all it will take to get me hooked again. I *never* long to join everyone else in the toast, or the glass of wine with my dinner, or down at the pub with my mates getting rat faced. I genuinely feel sorry for those people.

I get told that I'm not a real alcoholic! No shit! I stopped being an alcoholic the day I stopped putting the stuff in my mouth. Period.

If you want to stay an alcoholic, you can. You don't need to drink alcohol to be a victim of alcoholism. You can remain an alcoholic for the rest of your life, letting the one drink haunt you and keep you awake at nights. If you believe you're an alcoholic for the rest of your life, guess what: you Are!

By eliminating your wonky beliefs about alcohol, you also eliminate your desire for alcohol. You never crave something you don't want. If you find yourself craving alcohol, ask yourself which beliefs you're still holding onto?

When you accept that your beliefs sculpt all your thoughts and your thoughts construct all your beliefs, you'll have no problem in taking 100% responsibility for all your actions. This acceptance helps you see that nobody ever forced you to take one single drink, never mind the thousands that it took for your drinking to become the 'problem' it's become right now.

Accepting 100% of the responsibility is not a way of assigning blame. You can't do anything about what's happened in the past. It's done and dusted. The only part of your past that you can change is how you think about it in the present moment. It's time to move on.

Your Ability to Respond

What happens now depends on how you see your ability to respond. You can only respond in the here and now. This is the only time you have, and the only time you can respond. You can't alter the past and you don't have a crystal ball to predict what's going to happen tomorrow or the next day, and so on. You can only make your choices and take your actions right now in this moment.

Not so long ago, I listened to a recording of the Dalai Lama speaking about his interpretation of the idea of karma. I'm not a religious person, by any stretch of the imagination, but there's just something about this guy that makes sense to me.

In this particular recording, he said that karma was the cumulative sum of all your thoughts and actions. Where you are right now in this moment is the sum total of every thought that you've ever had and every action that you've ever taken. In short, karma means that you are the product of your own past thoughts and actions, and nothing else.

The more I thought about it, the more I could see karma as an elemental truth. Forget about the moral significance or the religious connotations for a minute. Just look at it from the perspective of your own personal history. You are what you are because of who you are and what you've done. You've nobody to blame but yourself!

For me, the eureka moment came when he spoke about future karma. He said your personal future karma will also be the sum of all your present thoughts and actions. So you have the chance to put things right! The decisions and the choices that you make right now in this very moment are the ones that will build the person you will become in your future. Isn't that an excellent thought? You can start to reverse any and all negativity from your past by changing your thoughts and actions in the present. Each moment you live by this philosophy, you move yourself into a better, brighter future.

The Dalai Lama was speaking about karma in neither good nor bad terms. There was no aspect of moral judgment attached to anything he was saying, as in good or bad karma. There was no hint of looking back to your past and feeling ashamed or guilty about your previous thoughts or actions. On the contrary, the message was that you can profit from understanding the mistakes you've made in your past, and through learning from those mistakes, not repeat them. Your past is your friend, not your enemy. Learning gives you the chance to put things right. If more people learned from the lessons of the past, the world might be a better place.

You might hold the belief that alcohol is a part of your culture. You might think you have the 'alcoholic gene' or that you drink because your family drank. If you look at how your life has got to where it is now, through this interpretation of karma, you can see that you are the collective result of all your thoughts and actions. What does that say about your alcohol problem?

It tells you that your problem with alcohol is, ultimately, YOUR problem.

Where you will be one year from now depends on what you do right now. How you behave in this moment dictates the direction of your future. It's not about the actions you take in five minutes or an hour or next week, but the actions you take right now in this moment.

If you delay quitting until you get to a future self that you think is a more capable, stronger version of you, it will never happen, and you'll never quit. At this moment in time, that stronger version of you only exists in your head. Bringing that person out of your thoughts and into reality takes action, and you can only take those decisive actions right now. The stronger version of you cannot magically appear. That person has to be built by you, bit by bit, action by action. If you don't build the better you, it will always remain a dormant and useless thought stuck in your mind, and nothing more.

Remember, this is where you are now. You can never be anywhere else but where you are in this moment. And this is the only time you ever get to do anything at all.

If you make the choice to use alcohol right now, of course it's your choice to make. But your future self will be the one to bear all the consequences!

Your Mind Trusts What You Tell It - So Talk Nice

"We can complain because rose bushes have thorns, or rejoice because thorn bushes have roses."
Abraham Lincoln

Positive Thinking

In the quote from the beginning of this chapter, Lincoln had it right. We can complain about how tough it is to be without alcohol, how much we're missing the buzz, or how crappy our lives will be now that we can't enjoy a party any more. Or we can celebrate how great it is to finally rid ourselves of this poison and congratulate our wisdom on seeing past the propaganda and nonsense. Who do you think is going to have the easier life at the end of the day?

When you're quitting drinking, positive thinking and self-talk is not only desirable, it's absolutely essential, in my opinion. This is especially true in the early days. Thinking positively means more than just telling yourself that you can do this. Positive thinking has to be coupled with positive action. You can talk positive until the cows come home, but nothing will come of it unless you do something decisive with all that positive energy.

You also need to have a positive plan for the actions you're going to take, which we'll look at in the final chapter, and you need to consistently follow that plan. Without a plan, you are just drifting aimlessly, without a clear-cut-direction.

Negative Thinking

Negative thinking will only keep you locked into your old beliefs. If you constantly tell yourself that you can't do it, you will find ways to fail. As soon as you get to the first hurdle, you'll feel like giving up. How can you change any bad habit when you persistently undermine your own efforts by bitching at yourself, telling yourself that you're no good, that you won't be able to put up with this or that, or telling yourself how bad things are going to get, while at the same time harking back to how it used to be in the 'good old days'?

Negative self-talk casts a cloud over your future where the only light you can see is how things were in your past. If the only goodness you can see in the world is where you've come from, you're not going to be too thrilled about taking too many steps in the opposite direction.

The How-To

How do you keep yourself positive?

The first step to overcoming negative self-talk is to become aware that you're doing it. In the first few days after quitting, you will be in a heightened state of awareness. Don't forget, your mind is now alcohol-free. This poison is no longer interfering with those delicate chemical balances that are vital for healthy brain function. Therefore, your thinking will be much clearer.

Another aspect of staying positive is to focus on one thing at a time. Don't take on too much at once. Talking shite to yourself probably spans many areas of your life. For the time being, your job is to focus on the shite self-talk surrounding your alcohol use. This makes your task of becoming aware of your shite self-talk a little easier. Later, when you've gained your alcohol freedom, you can deal with the other areas of shite self-talk that are messing with your head!

Listening to the Inner Voice

We all have an inner voice, chattering away in the background for most of our waking hours. You need to listen to what this voice is saying because, as we've seen, those words can influence your actions. What are you listening for? You're listening for statements like "I can't do it", "I don't feel like it", "I'm not good enough", or "It's just too hard".

These thoughts are going on in the background, often without you being aware that they're even happening. Just because you aren't aware of them doesn't mean you aren't being influenced by them. Some of your most influential thoughts and feelings are happening at this subconscious level. You can't do squat about your negative put-downs unless you're aware of them. And there's no other way of becoming aware of what you're saying to yourself than actively listening to your inner voice.

Listening in the moment is easy. If I asked you what you are thinking right now, you could pretty much give me a rough idea. That's because you are focusing your full attention onto your thoughts. But in the long run these thoughts are pushed into the background. You need to remind yourself to think about your thinking.

Put sticky notes up all over your home and work, reminding yourself to listen and keep your thoughts positive. Again, being listening to your self-talk is one of the first steps in changing it.

Changing Your Inner Voice

Have you ever noticed how your negative voice sounds? Another thing you can try is the change the tone, pitch, and even the entire person behind those inner negative voices. My inner moaner sounds like a whiny, spoiled child. It's always complaining, bitching, carping on about how I'm not good enough, how I should just accept who I am and where I came from, and how this is all there's ever going to be. You might have experienced something similar.

Although this voice seems like it has complete reign over your thoughts, it doesn't. It's entirely under your control. Once you change the voice, you change the effect it has on you. It's a bit like the old trick of picturing someone you're nervous about meeting, sitting on the toilet with their pants down. Seeing someone in this way puts the dynamics back into perspective. They're just like you, and nothing to be scared of.

In a similar fashion, as soon as you hear the whinny, bitchy, negative voice in your head, take away its negative sting by altering the voice. Give it a super sexy voice like Betty Boo or Jessica Rabbit. Imagine sexy Jessica saying "It's just too hard!" Alternately, give it the voice of Homer Simpson, Goofy, or Daffy Duck.

Homer's my favorite. When the nasty self-talk is punctuated by a series of 'Doh's', it makes it very difficult not to smile.

Hype up these voices to make them sound silly. Exaggerate the hell out of them. The more you can magnify the ludicrous, the better. How can you take your whiny bitchy inner voice seriously when it really sounds like such a lame dumbass?

Remember that it's all under your control. You choose whether to give power to the negative voices or not.

Alcohol Freedom Mindset Seven

The Key To an Awesome Future is in Your Personal Life Blueprint

"You are never too old to set another goal or to dream a new dream."
C. S. Lewis

Quitting Drinking as a Goal

If you treat quitting drinking alcohol as a goal, you'll likely hit a brick wall once you've stopped. Not doing something isn't much of a goal in and of itself. How many things can you think of that you're not going to do today? I'm not going to figure skate today! I'm not going to climb Mount Everest or go to the moon today. I'm not going to give up alcohol today. How can you define yourself by the things you don't do?

You don't have to do anything to stop drinking. Once you don't put alcohol in your mouth again, you've achieved what you set out to achieve, and your goal is reached. If you decide right now to stop drinking alcohol and you never touch another drop again, guess what? You've done it...! Congratulations!

The Opportunity Costs of Alcohol Use

As we've seen, your alcohol use has prevented you from doing a lot of the positive things that you could have been doing with your life. While you've been using alcohol, high on alcohol, or coming down from that alcohol high, there has always been the opportunity cost of what might have been. And these opportunity costs mount up pretty quickly, adding up to a whole heap of missed opportunities over the space of just a month or a year.

I drank for over 30 years! I don't even want to think about my personal opportunity costs.

Where Do You Want to Take Your Life?

Now that your alcohol-drinking is in the past (congratulations again, by the way!) you can turn your back on that past and concentrate on your future. What do you see in the personal future you wish for? When I stopped I had a vague idea about what I wanted to do. Be healthy, be a good role model, make some more money, have an easier life, buy the dream car, build the dream house, and so on.

When you're a heavy drinker it's difficult to effectively follow through and succeed at anything you plan.

I never had a problem coming up with ideas or plans. I could lay out what I wanted to do, how I was going to carry out those plans step by step, and what it would look like once I got there. Then I'd have a drinking session which might last a couple of days. I'd take another couple of days to recover. And before I knew it, a week was gone and my plan was either postponed or put very much onto the back burner. Eventually I gave up making anything but half-hearted plans.

There's a reason why drug addicts are not, by and large, successful people. They have a short supply of quality time to make themselves successful.

Finally, at the end of 2012, I made the decision to quit and I stopped drinking alcohol forever.

BAM!

Suddenly I had lots of time on my hands.

As the weeks went by, the quality of that time got better and better. The barriers of entry to my new life were swiftly disappearing. I found that if I made a plan to do something, it generally got done! I made more plans. I made better plans. I made more complex plans. Each time the plans got done.

It's been two years since I drank my last dribble of alcohol and I can safely say that this has been the most productive time in my entire life. I'm learning something new every day. My confidence in myself and in my abilities to do things is at an all-time high. This is my second book, and I'm already half way through the first draft of my third. I've made over 250 self-help videos for AlcoholMastery.com, written hundreds of posts, and started a new podcast. Without drinking alcohol, I feel like I can achieve anything!

I'm not saying any of this to boast. Everything I tell you is to instill the belief in you that if I can do it, so can anyone, and so can you. I've always had it in me to write. When I was a boy, I always dreamed of being a science fiction writer. Although my life didn't take that direction, I got back to writing a few years ago when I was looking for an alternative to my forestry career. I started writing articles for other people, as what I call a 'working writer', trying to put bread on the table. But I never had the belief in myself to put my heart and soul into any of my writing. That is until I stopped drinking.

Stopping using this drug has opened my mind and made me believe that I can do this and much more. That's why I place such a high emphasis on planning goals in your life, not just the goal of quitting drinking, but goals that will stretch your mind and put you on the path of your dreams. As corny as that sounds, it's true. I don't care who you are or what you're capable of. You will never function to the best of your abilities if you are saturating your body and brain with a chemical that constricts and destroys the very organ that gives you those abilities in the first place. When you put alcohol into your body you give yourself a handicap. The more alcohol you drink, the more severe that handicap will become.

Above all, I've become a good influence on my son. If there was no other personal benefit to me stopping drinking, that would be enough.

The Windshield Effect

Richard Branson talks about focusing on what's in front of you right now instead of wasting energy worrying about your past. He calls this the windshield effect. In a nutshell, to move forward in life, you must put most of your concentration and focus on the road ahead. At the same time, you need to be aware of the things that are in your rear view mirror, understanding and accepting them as part of your journey. You can and should learn about your past, but your future is out there in front of you.

Where does *your* future lead? What is your plan?

Creating Your Personal Life Blueprint

Many people go through their whole lives without a goal or a plan. They may have plenty of expectations, but no real idea about how they are going to turn those expectations into reality. Is that a good way to lead your life?

Before we depart for our vacations, for instance, we have to make detailed plans. We know what time we'll leave home, which direction we're going to take to get to the airport, what time the plane leaves, how we'll get from the airport to our final destination once we've landed, and maybe a plan of what we're going to do when we arrive, even if it's no more than to lay on the beach until we turn bright red.

The most successful people tend to plan every part of their lives with great attention and focus on the details. They look at where they want to be in five or ten years' time. Then they work backwards, figuring out how they are going to reach that destination. They know what they need to do this year to get one step closer to that ten year goal. They also know what they need to do every month to reach their targets at the end of each year, and what they need to do day by day if they are going to get to their monthly goals.

Facing Towards Your Future

What are your goals? What has using alcohol stopped you from doing or thinking? What do you want to do, now that you don't drink alcohol anymore? These are the things you should be focusing your attention on.

Your objective is to put as much distance between your old alcohol soaked life and your new alcohol-free life, and to do it as quickly as you can.

From here on out - you don't use alcohol any more, you're not an alcoholic or an alcohol user, and alcohol is nothing more than a torn page from your own history book.

Now, you're going to focus your energies on your future.

"Your attitude, not your aptitude, will determine your altitude!" Zig Ziglar

What do you want to do in the next five or ten years?

What strong relationships do you want?

Who do you want to be with?

What job or business would you like to do?

How much money do you want to be earning?

The possibilities are endless for the things you can achieve now that you're not wasting your life, poisoning yourself with this poisonous, time-wasting drug!

Good luck and bon voyage!

Onwards and Upwards!

Please Consider Leaving a Review for Alcohol Freedom

Before you go, I would like to thank you for purchasing this Book.

Now that you've finished reading *Alcohol Freedom*, I'd like to ask you for a *small* favor. Would you be kind enough to help spread the word by leaving an amazon review.

Your feedback helps me to continue writing the type of books that help you to achieve the results you want. If you loved the book, please let me know :)

To submit a review:

Go to the *Alcohol Freedom* product page on Amazon.com.

Click on the 'Write a customer review' in the Customer Reviews section.

Click Submit.

$5 Discount Alcohol Freedom Audiobook

As a thank you for purchasing this paperback, I would like to give you a **$5 discount off** the audiobook version. Simply go to this link selz.co/1xsEWAD and enter the code: **NTQQLS8D** into the discount field. You can download and listen to the audiobook instantly... Thank you and enjoy!

More Information About Quitting Alcohol

If you would like more information about quitting alcohol you can visit our website at: alcoholmastery.com

At the time of writing there are over 300 free videos for you to choose, from many alcohol quitting related topics.

You can also listen to our regular podcast on iTunes by going to iTunes and searching for Alcohol Mastery.

If you have any questions or topics you would like to see featured on the podcast or in the videos, please contact me. My email is kevin@alcoholmastery.com.

Onwards and Upwards!

Free Alcohol Mastery Newsletter

You can get our free newsletter at the website – alcoholmastery.com. Just enter your first name and email address in the small form located in the sidebar.

Other Books by Kevin O'Hara

How to Stop Drinking Alcohol - A Simple Path From Alcohol Misery To Alcohol Mastery

Available on Kindle or Paperback

eBook on Amazon.com

Paperback on Amazon.com

You can also get the Audiobook by going to this page selz.co/1xsEWAD ... Don't forget your $5 discount off... see the audiobook page!

Made in the USA
San Bernardino, CA
29 December 2017